Buyer's Price Guide

ENGLISH PORCELAIN

Compiled and Edited

by

Judith H. Miller, M.A.

Consultant Editor

Gordon Lang, Sotheby's

mJm
PUBLICATIONS
Pugin's Hall
Finchden Manor
Tenterden
Kent
telephone 058 06 2234

The Publishers would like to acknowledge the
great assistance given by:

Anderson and Garland, Market
Street, Newcastle-upon-Tyne.
Bonhams, Montpelier Street,
London, S.W.7.
Bygones, Charing, Kent.
Charnwood Antiques, 65 Sparrow
Hill, Loughborough.
Christie, Manson & Woods Ltd.,
8 King Street, London.
Church Street Gallery, Church
Street, Tewkesbury.
Crispin Antiques,
10 The Broadway, Amersham.
Andrew Dando, Queen Square,
Bath.
John Francis, Thomas Jones &
Sons, King Street, Carmarthen.
Mendl Jacobs, The Antique Shop,
11 Ashford Road, Tenterden.
Lawrences, South Street,
Crewkerne.
Market Bosworth Antiques,
Market Bosworth, Nuneaton.
Morphets of Harrogate, 4-6 Albert
Street, Harrogate.

Mrs. M. K. Nielsen, Seaford House,
High Street, Moreton-in-Marsh.
Phillips Auctioneers, Blenstock
House, 7 Blenheim Street,
London, W.1.
Sotheby's Belgravia, 19 Motcomb
Street, London, S.W.1.
Sotheby Beresford Adams,
Watergate Street, Chester.
Sotheby King & Chasemore,
Pulborough.
Sotheby Parke Bernet & Co.,
34-35 New Bond Street,
London, W.1.
Studio Antiques,
Bourton-on-the-Water.
Melvyn Traub, Grays Antique
Market, 58 Davies Street,
London, W.1.
Whytock and Reid, Sunbury
House, Belford Mews,
Edinburgh.
Woolley and Wallis, Castle Street,
Salisbury.

Made and Printed in Great Britain by

Robert MacLehose, Scotland

CONTENTS

Introduction

ENGLISH PORCELAIN

This specialist price guide to English Porcelain illustrates, describes and realistically evaluates nearly 600 items covering examples from the early days of porcelain production in the middle of the eighteenth century to some pieces from the early twentieth century.

The history of porcelain is a fascinating one. The Chinese discovered the secret of producing porcelain in the 8th century. It is amazing to think that it took over 1,000 years for the technique to be perfected in Europe. The height of the Chinese porcelain manufacture was achieved in the Ming dynasty 1368-1644, when a truly magnificent porcelain was produced, with a beautiful body and clear glaze. This was widely exported. The wealthy patrons in Europe began to prefer the fine imported white-bodied Chinese porcelains to the local pottery, stonewares, Delft, etc. All over Europe chemists were trying to find the formula for this new porcelain. The first European success at emulating the Chinese process is credited to Johann Friedrich Bottger. in 1708 he produced an excellent white hard paste porcelain at Albrechsburg castle near Meissen.

POTTERY v. PORCELAIN

The difference between pottery and porcelain is basically one of translucency. Pottery is opaque, whereas porcelain will transmit light. This, as with most bold statements of fact, has to be qualified. A thickly potted early Bow plate or bowl, for example, may not show much translucency, whereas there is some very fine pottery which one could almost claim to be transmitting light. However, as a general rule of thumb the translucency principle stands.

HARD PASTE AND SOFT PASTE

The Chinese, Japanese and most of the European factories produced hard paste porcelain. The English factories, in common with early Vincennes or Sevres produced soft paste porcelain. The difference between the two is quite crucial to one's identification of eighteenth century porcelain and understanding of this difference is best achieved by the constant handling of examples of both. In this case damaged pieces are, in fact, a great advantage. In general, hard paste porcelain is indeed 'harder' or 'colder' to the touch than soft paste, which appears 'warmer' and somehow more porous to the touch.

the glaze on hard paste tends to look quite cold and glittery, hence harder. Soft paste glaze looks softer and often slightly creamier. This is especially true on the earlier wares before the discovery that the addition of tin oxide whitened the glaze. Many glazes on soft paste were prone to crazing and some, particularly Bow, were prone to discolouration and staining.

Chips on soft and hard paste porcelain can reveal a great deal. On hard paste, which is quite brittle, a chip will appear glass like, with small points. On soft paste, a chip has a granular appearance and such chips frequently show staining, due to the more porous body.

Most 18th C. English factories produced soft paste porcelain, with the exception of Plymouth, Bristol (both of which are relatively rare) and Newhall. The plot thickens. Not only did some early 18th C. factories produce hard paste, but the type of soft paste varied considerably, according to area and availability of materials. Hence Bristol, Caughley and Worcester used a soapstone body; Bow, Lowestoft and Derby used a bone-ash body; Chelsea, Longton Hall nd early Derby used a glassy body. All these were overtaken in the 9th C. by English bone china which became the standard.

MARKS

A great deal of importance is placed on the identification of actory by reliance on marks. This s sheer folly. For one thing, much arly porcelain was unmarked, such displays only a workman's mark and some a copy of a Chinese mark, taken from the copied piece f export ware. Another point of onfusion was due to the common habit of copying marks from another factory. Another area of difficulty is the decorators who moved from one factory to the next, sometimes using the same mark. A Billingsley rose, for example, can enote not only Swansea and Nant-garw but also Derby, Pinxton or Worcester. A similar story can be old for James Giles exotic birds. The only true identification has to come from the porcelain body itself, using the mark purely as verification. Samson in the late 19th C. and 20th C. copied much 18th C. English porcelain, particularly Chelsea and Derby. This should however, pose no problems as he used a continental hard paste body.

DECORATION

The decoration on English porcelains falls into 4 main types: underglaze, overglaze, painted and printed. Most underglaze work was done in blue. It should be noted that when the 'blue' was applied to the unglazed porcelain, it was in fact black and the painter had to work out shading and different tones purely by experience. The true colour appeared only after firing. The blue and white designs, particularly on tewares, were for most English factories (with the possible exception of Derby and Chelsea), their main money makers. As the popularity of blue and white porcelain spread and demand increased, the printing process was employed to ensure a ready supply of popular patterns. Apart from the initial copper plate this could be done by almost totally unskilled labour. One should not dismiss printed wares as having no quality, many are crisp and competent and show the true skill of a master copper engraver. This is also the case for a large amount of the hand painted wares, as they were copied from established patterns and could be executed by apprentice painters, usually youngsters on very low pay.

The overglaze painting with enamels was generally perfected at most factories. Due to the lower firing temperature these wares were actually simpler to manufacture, having less kiln damage than the blue and white pieces. Overglaze printing was introduced in the English factories in the mid 1750's (at least 5 years before underglaze blue printing was introduced).

PRICE RANGES

In this volume we have concentrated on pieces which one would expect to find in antique shops and auction rooms rather than rare museum pieces which are normally well illustrated in the standard text books. The exceedingly rare pieces are very difficult to place within a price range and ones chance of finding such a piece is slim unless one is buying from a top international sale room. All items in this book are given a price range which gives a guide to the sort of price one must expect to pay for a similar piece, Condition is, of course, vital to any discussion of price, and this is particularly true with porcelain. Always check the piece very carefully and if unsure always buy from a reputable dealer or auction house. A dealer should be willing to provide a full invoice, stating approximate date and condition. One should always try to buy the best piece one can afford, rather than two or three damaged or indifferent pieces, especially if one is thinking in terms of investment. It is, however, also sensible to buy what you like rather than what you think you should like. You make fewer mistakes that way.

Bargains are still around and new 'finds' appear in salerooms and dealers shops all the time. Used sensibly, this book, with its dating and recognition hints and clear photographs, should prove invaluable to both the private buyer and professional dealer.

An Aynsley plate, signed by
R. Keeling, with fern jewelling,
c. 1890. **£120-140**
*Note typical lobed or fluted shape
of the 1880's/90's.*

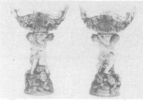

A pair of Bevington comports,
painted mark in underglaze-blue,
late 19th C., height
28.5 cm **£300-330**
*Both the form and mark of these
comports are straight copies of
(Dresden) Meissen neo-rococo
originals.*

BOW PORCELAIN

- probably the first porcelain
  factory in England
- although the date normally
  given for the opening of the
  factory is c. 1747, many experts
  now believe it was established
  much earlier c. 1744-45
- very similar body to early
  Lowestoft
- painter's numerals sometimes
  in footrings — another
  confusion with Lowestoft
- body heavy for its size and
  very porous, prone to
  discolourations
- translucency poor
- tended to warp in the kiln
- after 1765 quality markedly
  deteriorated
- not much Bow can be
  authenticated after the end of
  the 1760's
- factory closed in 1776

A pair of Bow candlestick-groups
emblematic of summer and
autumn, enriched with puce and
gilding, nozzles cracked, anchor
and dagger marks in iron-red,
c. 1765, 26 cm. high. **£750-900**

A pair of Bow bocage
candlesticks, on scroll moulded
bases, with four scroll feet,
enriched in gilt and turquoise,
repairs to candle nozzles, wings
of Cupids and one foot, chips to
flowering foliage, 28.5 cm. high,
iron-red anchor and dagger
marks, c. 1760. **£300-400**
*The rococo fashion of over
elaboration is evident in these
heavily encrusted groups
supported on assymetrical scroll
bases.*

A Bow shaped oval dish,
moulded with grapes and vine
leaves in low relief, all in enamel
colours, 25 cm., anchor and
dagger mark in red, mid 18th C.
slight chipping to rim. **£250-350**
*Dishes of very similar form were
produced at Derby
contemporaneously.*

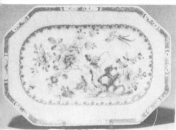

A pair of Bow famille rose dishes, painted with a phoenix in flight among pink and iron-red chrysanthemum, minute rim chips, 27.5 cm. wide, c. 1753. **£280-350**
Derived directly from a Chinese exportware (or Compagnie-des-Indes) original of the early Qianlong period.

BOW FIGURES

- the earliest Bow figures have plain bases
- in the mid 1750's some rococo bases appeared: these became more popular
- by 1760 C & S scroll decoration was in great demand as were large shell bases
- the large shell bases can be thought of as a trademark of Bow, although many other factories copied successful features
- very little Bow is marked
- anchor and dagger mark was added by James Giles when he painted a piece at the factory
- figures with an underglaze blue crescent tend to be Bow (although this was a Worcester mark, it was often copied by Bow and other lesser factories)

A Bow white figure of an itinerant bagpiper, pieces missing from hat and instrument and fingers, c. 1755, 22.5 cm. high. **£500-600**

A Bow shell sweetmeat dish, painted with bouquets of flowers in bright colours, 11.5 cm. high, c. 1755-60. **£330-400**
Similar sweetmeats were manufactured at Derby, Plymouth and Bow.

A pair of Bow white figures of Kitty Clive and Henry Woodward, in the roles of 'The Fine Lady' and 'The Fine Gentleman', restored, c. 1750, 25.5 cm. and 26.5 cm. high. **£1,200-1,400**
These figures are of heavy construction typical of early Bow.

An 18th C. Bow figure of autumn, square aperture at rear 5¼ in. high. **£200-250**
The square aperture for an ormolu mount at the back is a characteristic of Bow. Chelsea and Derby used a more or less circular aperture.

11

A Bow figure of a shepherd playing the bagpipes, chips and crack to stump, c. 1755, 26 cm. high. **£600-750**

A Bow figure of a seated bagpiper, slight chips to hat, 8½ in., c. 1758-60. **£700-900**

A Bow seated figure of a putto, symbolic of 'Winter' 6¾ in. **£150-£200**

A Bow figure of a nun, c. 1760, 6 in. high, should be reading a book, but if perfect **£600-670** *Chelsea, Longton Hall and Bow all produced figures of a monk and nun.*

A pair of Bow figures of a shepherd and shepherdess wearing pale pink and puce gilt flowered clothes, enriched in green and gilding, some minor chipping to flowers, anchor and dagger marks in iron-red, c. 1765 19 cm. high. **£600-800**

A pair of Bow figures, 'Water' and 'Air', from a set of the Elements, painted in enamel colours, height 26 cm., painted anchor and dagger marks, c. 1770, firing cracks. **£600-800** *Classically inspired figures are generally of less interest than figures of contemporary subjects.*

The Toppin pair of Bow cooks, the mound bases both applied with modelled flowers, variously painted, her head replaced from a different model, 17.5 cm. and 18 cm. **£700-900**

A Bow figure, c. 1765, 6 in. high, slight firing crack, anchor and dagger and Worcester mark. **£500-600**

A pair of Bow sheep, picked out in purple or brown, slight damage, height 8.6 cm., mid 18th C. **£150-180**

A small Bow coffee mug, painted in 'famille-rose' enamels with 'Chinese Peony' pattern, c. 1755. **£100-120**

A Bow blue and white cream jug, of squat pear shape, painted with the 'Golfer and Caddy' pattern, 3¼ in. painter's mark in blue, c. 1755, slight chip to foot, hairline crack at spout. **£200-£250**

A Bow figure of a green parrot, restoration to tail feathers and flowers, 5½ in. high, c. 1763-65. **£800-900**

A pair of Bow mugs, painted in the Chinese manner in underglaze blue, 12 cm., chip to one rim, c. 1752-55. **£300-500** *Imitations of Chinese exportware originals.*

A Bow bell-shaped mug, 14.5 cm. high, c. 1760. **£440-520**

An early Bow small plate, with iron-red decoration, transfer printed from the engraving by R. Hancock after Gravelot, within a scroll and ribbon surround, the rim with a band of stylised lappets, minor rim chips, 20 cm. diam., c. 1755. **£300-450**
Iron-red transfer printing was utilised almost exclusively at Bow.

A Bow plate, painted in Compagnie-des-Indes, 'famille-rose' palette, c. 1755. **£50-70**

A Bow blue and white octagonal plate, decorated with the 'Image' pattern, simulated Chinese marks on the back, c. 1756, 8¾ in. **£100-120**

A small Bow blue and white plate, decorated with the 'Jumping Boy' pattern, c. 1759, 6¼ in. **£140-160**

A pair of Bow blue and white sauceboats, painted in runny underglaze-blue between cell diaper bands and stiff leaf borders, 8½ in., c. 1760-65, one chipped and fire cracked. **£200-£250**

An early Bow sauceboat, on a flat unglazed base, the outside moulded with scales, painted in 'famille rose' enamels, 14 cm. long. **£350-500**

A Bow blue and white sauceboat heavily potted, with slight rim chip, 8 in., c. 1775. **£100-120**

A Bow toy tea and coffee service, painted in underglaze-blue, comprising: tea pot, sugar basin, 2 tea bowls, 4 coffee cups and saucers. **£2,000-2,200**

A pair of Bow small bottle vases, painted in the Kakiemon palette, enriched in gilding, the slender necks with a band of trellis in turquoise suspending foliage, one repaired, 14.5 cm. high, c. 1755. **£500-800**
Augustus, the Elector of Saxony, had a passion for Japanese porcelain. His Japanese palace, the 'Johanneum', housed numerous pieces of Kakiemon porcelain. Meissen and subsequently Chantilly, St. Cloud, Mennecy, Bow, Chelsea and Derby all followed the fashion to produce their own copies.

BRISTOL c. 1749-1742
- **first porcelain to be produced was the soft paste produced by Benjamin Lund from 1749-1752**
- **These porcelains are very rare but examples sometimes show the relief moulded 'Bristol' or 'Bristoll'**
- **mostly underglaze blue ware in Chinese style**
- **the glaze was tight fitting although it had a tendency to pool and bubble**
- **the blue often looks watery where it has run in the firing**
- **in 1752 Bristol 'secrets' were sold to Worcester**

A Champion's Bristol cup and saucer, with basket moulding and gilt rims, c. 1775. **£190-230**
The earliest English hard-paste porcelain was manufactured by William Cookworthy at Plymouth between 1768 and 1770, when the concern moved to Bristol. Richard Champion took over control in 1773 and production ceased in about 1781. Note the restrained neo-classical style of floral swags pendant from the border, leaving most of the surface bare. The basket work is derived from the Meissen factory.

A Champion's Bristol flared beaker vase, with a puce line border, the interior with a loop and double-dot-pattern rim, blue X mark, c. 1775, 13 cm. high. **£200-300**

A pair of Champion's Bristol figures of a boy and girl, his head repaired, lacks index finger, both dogs' hats with minor chips, c. 1775, 18 cm. high. **£1,000-£1,200** the pair

15

A Champion's Bristol armorial teacup, coffee cup, saucer and spoon, each with a coat of arms in iron-red and yellow, within a gilt scroll and foliage surround and painted in colours, the cups with entwined handles and gilt dentil rims, the shell-moulded spoon painted with flower-sprays, c. 1775. **£800-1,200**

CAUGHLEY

- factory ran from 1772-1799, when it was purchased by the Coalport management
- painted wares tend to be earlier than printed ones
- Caughley body of the soapstone type
- often shows orange to transmitted light, but in some cases can even show slightly greenish which adds to the confusion with Worcester
- glaze is good and close fitting, although when gathered in pools, may have greeny blue tint
- later printed wares with gilding are much less collectable
- main marks: impressed 'Salopian', 'S' was painted on hand-painted designs, 'S' was printed on blue printed designs, although an 'X' or an 'O' was sometimes hand-painted beside it, one of the most common marks was the capital C. Hatched crescents never appeared on Caughley, they were purely a Worcester mark
- Caughley is often confused with Worcester, they have many patterns in common e.g., 'The Fishermans' and 'Fence'

A pair of Caughley dessert plates, painted with chinoiserie plants and pierced rocks within a border of Chinese emblems and flowers, on a powder blue ground, 7 in., blue 'C' marks. **£220-270**

BRISTOL c. 1770-1781

- **William Cookworthy transferred his Plymouth factory to Bristol in 1770**
- **Champion took over the works in 1773**
- **the body had a tendency to slight tears and firing cracks**
- **greatly influenced by the Chinese and also Sevres and Meissen**
- **Bristol colours are sharp and gilding is of excellent quality**

A Caughley blue and white asparagus server, with 'Fisherman's pattern', c. 1775. **£45-55**

A Caughley miniature meat dish, painted in underglaze-blue with buildings on an island and sampans, within a panelled border, 10.3 cm., S mark. **£70-90**

A Caughley blue and white plate, hand painted, impressed Salopian mark, 8 in. diam., c. 1785-95. **£80-90**

A Caughley shell shaped dish, c. 1770, with slight repair: **£150-£170**, perfect: **£260-290**

A Caughley blue and white cabbage leaf jug, decorated with the 'Fisherman' pattern, mask lip and scroll handle, height 19 cm., late 18th C. **£140-160**

A Caughley blue and white jug, 7 in. high, c. 1795. **£90-100**

A Caughley cream jug, printed with flowers and butterfly, c. 1765. **£120-150**

A rare Caughley blue and white sauceboat, with painted decoration, in mint condition. **£100-120**

A Caughley blue and white sugar bowl and cover, printed with underglaze-blue floral sprays, 'S' mark in underglaze-blue to base, 4¼ in. high, c. 1780. **£100-130**

17

A Caughley tankard, with zig-zag fence pattern, 6 in. high, c. 1780. **£150-170**
A pattern also occurring on Worcester porcelain.

A Caughley blue and white tankard, printed with the 'parrot pecking fruit' pattern, c. 1775, 3¼ in., C mark. **£120-170**
Worcester also used this design.

A Caughley cylindrical mug, printed in blue with on one side 'La Peche' after Pillement, the reverse with 'La Promenade Chinoise', 6 in., S mark in blue, c. 1780. **£200-260**
Another design used at Worcester.

A Caughley 'Mansfield' pattern small teapot, printed in underglaze-blue, 5 in. **£130-200**
Another 'Worcester' design.

A Caughley blue and white teabowl and saucer, S marked, c. 1785. **£30-50**
Caughley derived much of their design inspiration from Chinese exportware. The illustrated example is very close to the oriental original, and in some cases it is almost impossible to differentiate the two without a fairly close inspection: i.e. check whether it is hard or soft paste.

A Caughley printed teabowl and saucer, c. 1785. **£50-60**

18

A Caughley 'Fisherman' pattern
teapoy and cover, 4½ in., c. 1795.
£100-120

CHAMBERLAINS
c. 1780's-1852

- **Robert Chamberlain and his son left the main Worcester factory in 1783**
- **initially they decorated porcelain on a free-lance basis, mainly for Thomas Turner of Caughley**
- **Chamberlain started producing his own porcelain in the early 1790's**
- **the early body of Chamberlain was hard-paste, very similar to Newhall**
- **pattern numbers were sometimes used after 1794**
- **in 1807 the Prince of Wales allowed the mark 'Porcelain manufacturers to his Royal Highness the Prince of Wales' to be used**
- **'Regent China' was introduced in 1811**
- **best period for Chamberlains 1810-1830**
- **in the early 1840's bone china was introduced and the firm merged with Flight, Barr and Barr in 1852**

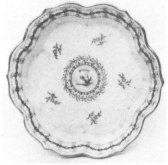

A Caughley part tea service,
each piece painted with a
medallion showing billing doves
beneath a label inscribed
'L'Amitie', comprising: teapot
and cover, teapot stand, tea
caddy and cover, milk jug, saucer
dish and two teabowls, c. 1790,
teapot cracked and chipped,
saucer dish cracked, tea caddy
knop damaged, one teabowl
chipped, slight rubbing. **£150-
£250**

A pair of Chamberlain's
Worcester yellow-ground
beakers, reserved on a brilliant
egg-yellow ground, gilt with
trailing strawberry flowers,
within gilt line rims, c. 1810,
10 cm. high. **£500-700**
*From about 1800-10 some of the
finest naturalistic painting to
appear on British porcelain
appears on Chamberlain's Flight
& Barr and slightly later on
Swansea and Nantgarw wares
executed by John Wood, Thomas
Baxter and Humphrey
Chamberlain.*

A Chamberlain's Worcester part
tea and coffee service, painted
with a Japan pattern, on salmon
and gilt trellis ground,
comprising: teapot and stand,
sugar basin, milk jug, bowl, 2
cake dishes, 7 tea cups, 7 coffee
cups and 6 saucers. **£200-250**
*The late Regency porcelains were
frequently decorated in Imari
style comparable to this example.*

CHAMBERLAIN'S

A Chamberlain's Worcester gold-ground part coffee-service, with a crest within the motto 'Nos Pascit Deus', 26 pieces, some damaged and repaired, the plates and cover with script mark, c. 1815. **£800-£1,000**

An important Chamberlain's Worcester cabinet plate, painted by Humphrey Chamberlain with Caesar's ghost appearing to Brutus in his tent near Sardis, signed H. Chamberlain Pinxt., the reverse inscribed Shakespeare's Julius Caesar, Act IV, Scene 3, 'Speak to me, what thou art . . .' marked 'Chamberlain's Worcester Porcelain manufacturers to H.R.H. The Prince Regent', 23.5 cm. **£250-400**

A Chamberlain's Worcester blue-ground part dinner service, comprising: a soup tureen, cover and stand, 4 sauce tureens, covers and stands, 2 vegetable dishes and covers, a two-handled circular bowl (cracked), 5 oval dishes in sizes, 17 soup plates and 36 dinner plates, impressed and printed marks. **£1,900-2,300**
The form of this service shows the more fluid forms of the neo-rococo period, which immediately followed the more restrained neo-classical movement fashionable at the end of the 18th C. and early 19th C.

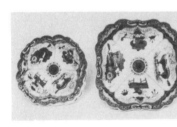

A part Chamberlain's Worcester dessert service, decorated with the 'Bengal Tiger' pattern, comprising: fluted saucer dish (First Period), two lozenge shaped dishes, 3 square dishes, a shell shaped dish, 10 plates and a coffee can and saucer, early 19th C., slight damage. **£200-400**
The 'Bengal Tiger' pattern originally appeared on Worcester of the First Period.

A pair of Chamberlain's Worcester urn-shaped ice pails, covers and liners, painted in a bright palette with the 'Bengal Tiger' pattern, reserved on coral-red and green seed-pattern grounds, minute chips to underside of handles, one cover with restoration to gallery, one cover with script marks and pattern no. 75, c. 1805, 31 cm. high. **£800-1,000**

A pair of Chelsea baluster finger bowls, with indented chocolate rims, both with very slight cracks to rim, one with minute rim chip, c. 1755, 7 cm. high. **£450-650**

One of a pair of Chamberlain's Worcester spill vases, inscribed 'Ceres' and 'Bacchante', Chamberlain's Worcester Manufacturers to their Royal Highnesses The Prince of Wales and Duke of Cumberland, c. 1807-10. **£300-400** pair
Probably painted by John Wood.

CHELSEA (soft paste porcelain) 1745-1784

- the finest English 18th C. porcelain
- earliest wares in milky white glassy porcelain
- Meissen inspired decorative style
- Transfer prints are extremely rare and are thought to have been done at Battersea enamel factory
- from 1749 Chelsea managed by Nicholas Sprimont a silversmith from Liege so style remained the same during red anchor period
- three small projecting 'spur marks' within a ground-down foot rim found on useful wares
- Chelsea figures beautifully modelled and colour used sparingly

A Chelsea pierced circular basket, the interior with a bouquet and flower-spray, the exterior with blue and yellow flowerheads, crack and restoration to foot, c. 1755, 16.5 cm. diam. **£250-350**
Baskets of similar form were made by the Lowestoft and Worcester factories.

A Chelsea teaplant beaker, in brilliant condition, in bright enamel colours and applied decoration, with apple sprig and insects inside and brown-edged rim, 3 in., c. 1745. Triangle period. **£1,000-1,200**

A Chelsea flared bowl and domed cover, the green twig handles with coloured flower terminals, cover cracked and damages to finial terminals, red anchor period, c. 1756 27.5 cm. wide. **£1,000-1,200**

CHELSEA

TRIANGLE PERIOD 1745-1749

- wares scarce and costly
- many based on silver prototypes
- many left undecorated
- if decorated generally in Kakiemon and Chinese style
- body comparatively thick, slightly chalky with 'glassy' glaze

A Chelsea clock case, modelled as a shepherd and shepherdess, in puce, pale-yellow and iron-red, surmounted by a rococo compartment to take a clock movement, she with restoration and some minor chips and repairs, gold anchor mark at back, c. 1765, 38 cm. high. **£850-£950**

A Chelsea oblong octagonal dish, with a moulded flowerhead pattern border and chocolate rim, c. 1752, 32.5 cm. wide. **£500-£600**

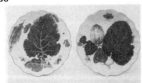

A pair of Chelsea candlestick-figures, emblematic of the four seasons, spring and summer as ladies, autumn and winter as gentlemen, minor chips, the nozzles later replacements, gold anchor marks, c. 1765, 27.5 cm. high. **£1,000-1,200**

A pair of Chelsea coffee-cups, painted with figures before ruins by a harbour, with chocolate line rims, both with slight damage to handles, one with minute crack and chips to rim and slightly crazed, red anchor marks, c. 1753, about 5 cm. high. **£450-£650**

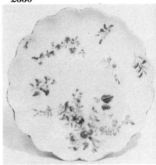

A pair of Chelsea fluted circular dishes, painted in soft coloured enamels, brown-edged rims, 7⅞ in., anchor marks in red, 1752-56. **£100-150**

A pair of Chelsea lobed circular dishes, painted with 'Hans Sloane' decoration, with brown-edged escalloped rims, 10½ in. and 10 in., red anchor marks. **£1,200-1,800**
The so-called 'Hans Sloane' plates were based on contemporary prints of botanical specimens.

CHELSEA

RAISED ANCHOR PERIOD
1749-1752

- paste now improved
- shapes still derived from silver, although Meissen influence noticeable
- mostly restrained decoration, either Kakiemon or sparse floral work (often to cover flaws)
- the most collectable ware of this period was fable decoration by J. H. O'Neale

A pair of Chelsea botanical dishes, painted in brilliant colours, with brown-edged rims, one with small hairline crack from rim, 21.5 cm. diam., brown anchor marks, c. 1755. **£1,300-£1,600**

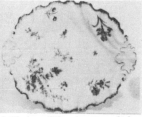

A Chelsea 'Silver' pattern dish, painted in coloured enamels within a green feathered edge, rubbed, 9½ in., red anchor period, 1752-56. **£150-200**

A pair of Chelsea silver-shaped dishes, with chocolate line rims, one rim with minute chip, one with red anchor mark, the other with 3 mark, c. 1755, 24.5 cm. wide. **£450-500**

A typical Chelsea dish based on a contemporary rococo silver shape. Note also the restrained academic style of the flower painting, this follows the fashion of Meissen's 'deutsche Blumen'. The German factory being at this time pre-eminent in Europe prior to the domination of the more flamboyant style of Sevres in the late 50's and 60's.

A Chelsea dish, a firing crack to the rim disguised by a leaf, red anchor mark, c. 1755, 34.5 cm. wide **£250-350**

GOLD ANCHOR PERIOD
1757-1769

- Chelsea's rococo period, with rich gilding and characteristic mazarine blue
- quite florid in style, in comparison to earlier more restrained painting
- influenced by Sevres
- elaborate bocage greatly favoured on figures
- has thick glaze which tends to craze

A pair of Chelsea lobed oval dishes, boldly painted with nuts, fruit and foliage, scattered butterflies and insects, within chocolate line rims, brown anchor marks, c. 1758, 33.5 cm. wide. **£700-900**

23

A Chelsea small dish from the Duke of Cambridge Service, painted in the atelier of James Giles in brilliant colours with fruit and foliage, enriched in gilding and turquoise, 21 cm. diam., anchor mark, c. 1763. **£700-1,100**
Compare with the Worcester 'Duke of Gloucester' Service, c. 1768-74.

RED ANCHOR PERIOD
1752-1756

- this period mainly influenced by Meissen
- glaze now slightly opaque
- paste smoother with few flaws
- the figures unsurpassed by any other English factory
- on useful wares, fine flower and botanical painting
- Chelsea 'toys' are rare and very expensive
- Chelsea is one of the few English factories to be collected by Continentals which has always kept the price buoyant
- Continentals particularly like the 'toys' and all products of the 'Girl in a Swing' Factory This was probably a small factory closely associated with the Chelsea factory. It was possibly only in existence for a few years in the late 1740's/early 1750's. Very few useful pieces have yet been attributed to the factory whose products are extremely rare and always expensive

A Chelsea peony dish, painted in colours, red anchor mark, c. 1755, 8 in. wide. **£600-700**

A Chelsea leaf dish, red anchor, c. 1752-56, 11 in. long. **£500-600**
Leaf dishes were popular at Chelsea, Derby, Worcester and Longton Hall.

A pair of Chelsea leaf dishes, the green twig handles with flower terminals, with chocolate line rims, flowers chipped, one cracked, red anchor mark, c. 1755, 27 cm. wide. **£350-450**
Dishes of similar form were manufactured at Meissen.

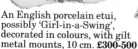

An English porcelain etui, possibly 'Girl-in-a-Swing', decorated in colours, with gilt metal mounts, 10 cm. **£300-500**

A rare Chelsea figure of a duck, restoration to tree stump and wing, 4¼ in. high, raised red anchor mark, c. 1750-52, restored: **£350-450**, if perfect: **£700-1,000**

A Chelsea figure of a lady musician, restoration to instrument, neck and waist, c. 1755, 15 cm. high. **£300-350**

A Chelsea figure of an ostler, right arm repaired, lacks left hand and fingers to right hand, slight chips to flowers, red anchor mark at front, c. 1755, 17 cm. high. **£700-1,000**

A pair of Chelsea figures of a gallant and companion, wearing puce and green and richly gilt flowered clothes, chips, other minor damages, gold anchor marks, c. 1770, 28 cm. high. **£1,300-1,500**

A pair of Chelsea sweetmeat figures, dressed in pale-yellow, turquoise, puce and iron-red flowered clothes, minor chipping to flowers, gold anchor marks, c. 1765, about 21 cm. high. **£800-£1,200**
Note the flowered dress and flower encrusted scrolled bases of the English rococo period.

A Chelsea figure of a pedlar, gold anchor period, c. 1765, 7½ in. high. **£300-350**

A Chelsea brown anchor plate, with fruit and moth decoration, c. 1758. 8 in. wide. **£300-400**

A red anchor Chelsea botanical plate, c. 1752-6, 8½ in. wide. **£270-300**

A pair of Chelsea plates, with shaped gilt rims, gold anchor marks, c. 1763, 22 cm. diam. **£600-700**

A pair of Chelsea strawberry-leaf moulded sauceboats, resting on four leaf-moulded feet with puce veins beneath a chocolate line rim, one with minor damage to terminal, red anchor marks, c. 1755, 20.5 cm. wide. **£1,100-£1,300**
Based on Meissen originals.

A Chelsea white acanthus leaf moulded milk jug, minute chip and crack to lip, traces of an incised triangle mark, 1745-47, 13.5 cm. high. **£3,500-4,000**
Early Chelsea wares were for th most part based upon silver originals and left in the white.

A pair of Chelsea plates, boldly painted with bunches of fruit, scattered fruit and a butterfly, with shaped chocolate line rims, minute rim chips, brown anchor marks, c. 1758, 21.5 cm. diam. **£350-450**

An attractive Chelsea sauce painted in a pale Kakiemon palette, raised anchor perioc c 1749-52. **£450-550**

A Chelsea octagonal teabowl and saucer, decorated with the 'Lady and Pavilion' Kakiemon pattern in green, red and blue enamels with gilt details, raised anchor period. **£700-900**

Like Bow, Chelsea copied Arita Kakiemon designs with remarkable accuracy. In the past there was frequent confusion between the Chelsea and Japanese examples, perhaps because both were fired on spurs and the palettes are for the most part similar. The more unctuous appearance of Chelsea porcelain of the period compares with the less sympathetic look of its oriental hard paste counterpart.

A Chelsea fable decorated teapot and cover, painted by O'Neale, some damage, red anchor mark, c. 1752, 18 cm. wide. **£5,500-£7,000**

A Chelsea baluster shaped teapot and cover, painted in puce, iron-red, green and yellow, the branch handle enriched in green and yellow, the cover and spout with chocolate rims, minute chip to tip of spout, 22 cm. wide, c. 1755. **£1,000-1,500**

A Chelsea cupid scent-bottle and stopper, the base mounted in gold and set with stone, restoration to quiver, c. 1755, 7.5 cm. high. **£1,000-1,200**

A Chelsea leveret tureen and cover, the cover with red anchor mark and 154, the base with 154, c. 1755, 9.5 cm. wide. **£1,000-£1,200**

A rare Chelsea 'billing doves' tureen and cover, with incised feather markings, enriched in puce, manganese, blue, green and iron-red, cover repaired, tureen cracked, 44 cm. long, red anchor period, c. 1755. **£2,000-2,500**

27

A garniture of three Chelsea pot pourri vases and pierced covers, painted in colours with exotic birds on fruiting branches, the domed covers and slightly flaring feet enriched in gilding, one small vase and cover restored, chips to flowers and foliage, 23.5 and 32 cm. high, gold anchor marks, c. 1765.
£500-700
A perfect example of English rococo, Note the asymmetrical scrolled form and flower-encrusted and pierced sides.

A 'Girl in a Swing' scent bottle and stopper, its plumage enriched in puce, brown and yellow, with white enamel and gilt collar inscribed 'Charmante', the base with gold mount, 1751-54, 6 cm. high. **£3,300-£3,600**

A Chelsea parasol handle, modelled with a youth's head wearing a grey hat with a red and yellow plume, restored, c. 1755, 11.5 cm,. long. **£320-400**

A pair of Chelsea Derby candelabra, for two lights each, 10¼ in. and 10½ in. **£600-800**

CHELSEA POINTS TO NOTE

- marks usually very small and not in prominent position
- paste varies from white to greenish when seen by transmitted light
- on red anchor ware, look out for 'moons' caused by frit in the kiln, also seen by transmitted light
- three spur marks often found on the base, left by kiln supports, also a feature of Arita porcelain (not to be confused with Derby pad marks)
- glaze on early pieces is reasonably opaque, this later becomes clearer and more glassy. Later still it becomes thicker when it tends to craze

A pair of Chelsea Derby two-handled covered cups and saucers, painted with sprigs and sprays of flowers in bright enamel colours, with rims and handles picked out in gold, anchor and 'D' mark in gold, late 18th C., very slight damage.
£200-300
The double-ogee sides and gilt dentil rims are a characteristic of this period.

A Chelsea Derby figure of a
sportsman, on scroll base picked
out in turquoise and gold, 8 in.,
patch marks, some restoration.
£120-150

A Chelsea scent bottle and a
stopper of 'Girl in a Swing' type,
base trimmed, neck damaged,
stopper a replacement, c. 1753,
10.5 cm. high. **£160-250**

A pair of Chelsea Derby figures
holding baskets, c. 1790,
restored, 5¼ in. high. **£250-300**

A rare Chelsea Derby inkstand,
the serpentine fronted base with
a raised and arched pen tray,
painted with scattered floral
sprigs and picked out in
turquoise and gilding, raised on
two claws and an acanthus scroll
foot, 21.4 cm. wide, 15 cm. high,
base incised 'N81', c. 1775, base,
inkwell and two knops damaged.
£200-400

A fine pair of Chelsea Derby
bucket-shaped jardinieres,
6½ in. wide, c. 1780. **£600-700**
*The French influence on these
jardinieres can be seen in the gilt
framed and lobed panel of
painting in the manner of
Boucher.*

29

A Chelsea Derby plate, slightly rubbed, early Imari style, c. 1760. **£100-120**

A Chelsea Derby figure of Neptune, 10 in. high, c. 1775, perfect: **£300-500**, with restored arm: **£250-300**

Eight Coalport (John Rose) custard-cups and covers on a tray, one a Derby (Samson Hancock) replacement, one handle riveted, the tray 40 cm. wide, c. 1810. **£550-700**

A Chelsea Derby teabowl and saucer, c. 1780. **£170-200**
Compare with the equally restrained style of Champion's Bristol who also produced similar lobed double-ogee forms.

COALPORT (Rose & Co.)

- factory was founded in the early 1790's by John Rose when he left Caughley
- Rose purchased the Caughley works in 1799 and ran them until he had them demolished in 1814
- produced hard-paste porcelain certainly after 1800, before then produced soapstone porcelain, this was quite similar to Caughley but does not have the yellow-brown translucency
- early wares heavy, with greyish appearance
- in this period quite similar to Newhall and Chamberlains
- in this period the highly decorated Japan wares have great quality as do some of the flower painted examples
- in around 1811 firm taken over by John Rose, William Clark and Charles Maddison
- in 1820 a new leadless glaze was invented and they also began to use Billingsley's fritt paste

A Coalport chocolate cup with cover and saucer, heavily embossed with flowers, c. 1830-45. **£300-350**

A Coalport (John Rose) sea-green ground part dessert-service, 40 pieces, some damaged, restored or replaced, c. 1810. **£2,900-3,200**

- in 1820 Rose also bought moulds from Nantgarw and Swansea and Billingsley came to work at Coalport
- best period for the Coalport factory began in 1820 when the factory produced a brilliantly white hard felspar porcelain, with a high level of translucency
- in terms of translucency and whiteness Coalport can be said to compete with Swansea and Nantgarw — although the factory never quite achieved the sheer brilliance of the Welsh factories and the potting is slightly heavier
- Coalport is often mistaken for Rockingham
- after 1820 CD, CD monogram, C.Dale, Coalbrookdale and Coalport were all marks used, before this date the marks tend to vary and much was unmarked
- in 1840's and 1850's Coalport perfected many fine ground colours: maroon, green and pink
- these often rivalled Sevres especially in 1850's and 1860's
- Coalport also at this time produced some Chelsea copies, with fake marks — these are very rare
- the Coalport factory is still in existence today

A good Coalport bowl and cover, painted and applied with naturalistically coloured and delicately modelled garden flowers, minor chips, 12.5 cm. over handles, c. 1840. **£150-200** . *A characteristic piece of 'revived' or neo-rococo porcelain, popular at both Coalport and Minton throughout the 1830's and early 40's.*

A Coalport (John Rose) bombe flower pot and pierced cover, lightly enriched in gilding, c. 1810, 29 cm. wide. **£200-230** *Note the realistic or naturalistic style of flower painting mentioned already in connection with the Worcester factories.*

A Coalport teacup and saucer, each piece painted with a group of brightly-coloured birds perched on branches within a gilt reserve, on a mazarine-blue ground. **£25-30**

A 9 piece Coalport dessert service, each piece printed and painted by P. Simpson, signed, printed mark, title and retailer's mark for Harrods, London, painted pattern number 9192/a, 22.4 cm., early 20th C. **£200-250**

A Coalport pot pourri jar and cover, profusely painted and gilded on a deep blue ground, printed mark, late 19th C., 33 cm. **£360-400**

A pair of Coalport (John Rose) claret-ground ice-pails, covers and liners in the Chelsea style, edged with gilt scrolls, one liner damaged, finials restored, c. 1810, 26 cm. high. **£650-800** *Although described as Chelsea style, this decoration originated at Sevres.*

A Coalport plate, from the service presented to Tsar Nicholas 1 of Russia by Queen Victoria, raised gilt decoration on blue ground, printed mark of the retailers A. B. & R. P. Daniell, 25 cm. **£550-650**

One of 6 Coalport (John Rose) armorial dinner-plates, the centres with arms and motto 'Libertas', 24 cm. diam., c. 1810. **£500-600** for six

A Coalport hand-painted plate, c. 1850, 9½ in. diam. **£135-165**

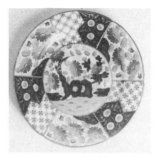

A Coalport plate, overhang 2 mark, c. 1810, 8½ in. **£60-80** *Note the typical six lobed form of early Coalport plates.*

A Coalport plate, with landscape decoration, c. 1860. **£145-165**

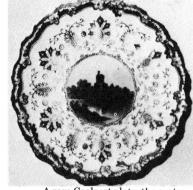

A rare Coalport plate, the centre with a view of Caistor Castle, decorated and signed by Perry, c. 1900. **£295-320**

A Coalport claret-ground racing trophy and cover, inscribed 'Pains Lane Races Sept 27th. 1853', the cover gilt with a band of trailing vine, 29 cm. high. **£900-1,100**

A good Coalport dessert plate, painted by F. H. Chivers, signed, on a turquoise-blue ground, rim with raised gilding, 9 in., printed crown mark, numbered 7218 and 54, impressed numerals, probably as date code for 1908. **£150-200**

A Coalport 'Felspar' tea service, comprising: a teapot, cover and stand, a milk jug, a sugar basin and cover, a bowl, a cake plate, 6 cups and 6 saucers, some damage, saucer: 14.7 cm., printed Society of Arts mark, c. 1830. **£250-300**
A typical neo-rococo tea-service often mistaken for Rockingham porcelain.

An unusual Coalport vase of Sevres inspiration, with a 'rose-Pompadour' ground, the scroll-moulded feet with gilt details, hair crack in base, 25 cm., gilt ampersand mark, 1860's. **£200-£300**

33

A Coalport slipper, decorated in gilding with a royal-blue ground, the interior also gilt, 14.5 cm., printed crown mark, c. 1890. **£200-250**

A Coalport part tea and coffee-service, painted with scenes from the life of Dr. Syntax, within pale apricot and blue borders edged with gilt key-pattern and panels of scrolls, comprising: a teapot, cover and stand (spout restored), a sugar-bowl and cover (base cracked), a milk jug, a slop-basin, 2 saucer-dishes (one cracked), 6 teacups (two cracked and one restored), 8 coffee-cups and 8 saucers, pattern no. 841, c. 1825. **£800-1,000**

An unusual Coalport vase and cover, the whole with a blue-green ground and gilt details, 39 cm., gilt CBD mark, c. 1851-61. **£120-180**

A Coalport vase, on pink ground with hand painted landscape, c. 1875, 6¼ in. high. **£150-200**

A Coalport 'jewelled' vase, painted by P. Simpson, signed with monogram, on a gilt band with turquoise enamel dots, 5½ in., printed crown mark, numbered V5955/m/s, 162, painted title, c. 1905. **£250-300**

A pair of Coalport vases and covers, with gilt borders of mottled pink and green over gilt flecks, 18 cm., printed crown mark, numbered V6470, c. 1910. **£270-330**

A good and large Coalport vase and cover, painted by J. H. Plant, signed with Jedburgh Abbey, with shaped royal-blue and gilt 'tortoiseshell' cartouches reserved on the cream ground, hair cracks to neck, knop restored, 41.5 cm., painted title and V5368, printed mark, c. 1910. **£400-500**

A Coalport 'named view' vase and cover, painted with a view of Harlech Castle, signed by Bud within raised gilt borders, reserved on a blue ground, pedestal base, 9¾ in., blue printed mark. **£150-250**

A Copeland plate, pierced rim with gilt, 9 in., c. 1890. **£150-190**

A pair of late 19th C. Copeland candlesticks, in Imari palette, 5½ in. high. **£70-80**

A pair of Davenport shallow bowls, enclosed by a shaped green-lobed rim, 27.5 cm., printed pennant and anchor mark, painted pattern number 233, c. 1850. **£120-150**

A pair of Copeland vases, in Sevres style, within raised gilt borders, reserved on pink and green grounds, 8¾ in., printed mark in green, c. 1900. **£200-£300**

35

DAVENPORT

An English porcelain toilet set, probably Copeland, painted with orchids in yellow, green and puce enamels, signed W. Birbeck, comprising: a jug and basin, chamber pot, toothbrush holder and soap dish and cover, late 19th C., slight damage. **£100-150**

DAVENPORT

- factory ran from 1793-1887
- early porcelain of a hard-paste variety
- any Davenport marked 'Longport' is quite rare
- high quality wares produced, particularly in the 1840's-1860's
- on botanical wares if the flowers are named it can add 50% to the value
- high quality Davenport often wrongly classified as Rockingham
- Davenport produced the Imari styles better known on Royal Crown Derby; this is rarer than Derby but not as highly collectable

A Davenport teapot, decorated, with a view of Lichfield Cathedral, c. 1860, 4¼ in. high. **£200-250**

A Davenport cup and saucer, in Persian style, puce mark, c. 1870. **£50-60**

An unusual Davenport cup and saucer, in Minton style, blue marked, c. 1860. **£50-60**

A Davenport cabaret set, the tray painted in colours with a view of 'Lake of Walenstad, Switzerland' by T. H. Barlow, signed on the front and named and initialled on the back, comprising: teapot and cover, sugar basin and cover, milk jug and two cups and saucers on an oblong tray, the saucers and tray with impressed mark Davenport. **£150-200**

A Davenport teacup and saucer, c. 1840. **£45-50**

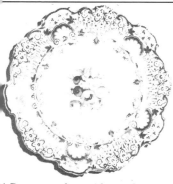

A Davenport plate, with raised
gilding, c. 1830-45. **£90-110**

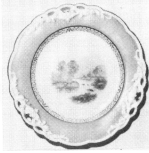

A Davenport plate, blue anchor
mark, c. 1860. **£60-70**

18th C. DERBY

- some early white jugs incised
  with the letter 'D' have been
  attributed to the Derby factory
  under the direction of John
  Heath and Andrew Planche,
  believed to start c. 1750
- early Derby is soft paste and is
  lighter than Bow and Chelsea
- very rare to find crazing on
  early Derby, the glaze was
  tight fitting and thinner than
  Chelsea
- glaze often kept away from the
  bottom edge or edge was
  trimmed, hence the term 'dry-
  edge'
- c. 1755 three (or more) pieces of
  clay put on bottom of figure to
  keep it clear of kiln furniture,
  giving 'patch' or 'pad' marks —
  which appear darker
- Duesbury had joined Heath
  and Planche in 1756
- Duesbury early works display
  quite restrained decoration,
  with much of the body left
  plain
- the porcelain of this period has
  an excellent body, sometimes
  with faintly bluish appearance
- Chelsea — Derby figures
  almost always made at Derby
- 1770's saw the introduction of
  unglazed white biscuit Derby
  figures
- 1780's Derby body very smooth
  and glaze white, the painting
  on such pieces was superb,
  particularly landscapes and
  flower painting

A Derby D-shaped bough-pot,
slight crack beneath one handle,
crown, crossed batons, and D
mark in iron-red, Duesbury &
Kean, c. 1805. **£250-300**
*'D' shape or demi-lune bough
pots were a very popular form in
the early years of the 19th C.
Other factories using this form
included Coalport,
Chamberlain's and Pinxton. Note
the distinctive Derby ram's
masks.*

A Derby bough pot and cover,
painted probably by George
Robertson, with peach coloured
ground gilded, the rim and base
picked out in canary yellow and
gilding, 24.7 cm., blue enamelled
crown and crossed batons mark
and inscription 'Near Bothwell
Castle, Scotland', brown
enamelled gilder's number '2',
possibly by Stables, c. 1796-1800.
£400-600

A Derby bough-pot and pierced cover, of bombe form, painted in the manner of Jockey Hill with 'Near Wirksworth, Derbyshire' (cracked round side), crown, crossed batons and D mark and inscribed in blue, Duesbury & Kean, c. 1795-1800, 19 cm. wide.**£200- 250**
Fundamentally a Sevres shape of the 1760's.

A pair of Derby cornucopia, painted by William Slater, Senior, 11.5 cm., red printed crown over Gothic 'D' mark, c. 1830. Restored: **£500-600.** If perfect: **£700-1,100**

A pair of Derby candlestick figures, with pierced scroll bases, Cupid's wing missing, 6½ in., c. 1770. **£200-300**
Derby's answer to the rococo products of Bow & Chelsea.

A pair of Derby flared flower-pots and two-handled stands, painted in the manner of Richard Dodson, crown, crossed batons and D marks in iron-red, Robert Bloor & Co., c. 1815, about 19 cm. high. **£700-800**

A pair of Derby yellow ground flared flower-pots, painted in the manner of George Robertson with 'At Panmure in Angushire, Scotland' and 'Near Inverness, Scotland', crown, crossed batons and D marks in blue, Duesbury & Kean, c. 1800, 13 cm. high. **£650-800**

A Derby comport, painted by John Brewer, 'Heliathus Multiflorus', blue mark, c. 1795, 12 in. wide. **£250-350**
Botanical subjects were popular at Derby.

A pair of Derby candlestick figures, painted in pale yellow, pink, purple, iron-red and turquoise, enriched in gilding, some restoration and chips to flowers, one nozzle branch restored, c. 1765, about 25 cm. high. **£1,000-1,200**

A Derby powdered-purple ground octagonal coffee cup and saucer, the saucer in black and gold, blue enamel crossed swords and gilt 29 marks, c. 1780. **£1,500-2,000**
An attempt to copy the late Baroque style of early Meissen.

A Derby coffee can and saucer, in dark blue ground with gilding and rare flower. Gilders:– saucer: Munday Simpson, coffee cup: Thomas Till, c. 1810-20. **£500-£560**

A Derby coffee can and saucer, with dark blue ground, decorated with matching Scottish scenes. **£300-400**

A Derby pale salmon pink ground coffee can and saucer, the can with slight crack to base of handle, the saucer with slight rubbing to gilding, crown, crossed batons and D marks and pattern No. 365 in puce, Duesbury & Kean, 1795-1800. **£1,200-1,500**

A Derby cup and saucer, by Zachariah Boreman, pattern 86, c. 1770, puce mark. **£700-800**

A Derby cup and saucer, with hand painted flowers, c. 1780, blue marked. **£170-200**
Compare this restrained neo-classical decoration with Champion's Bristol and slightly earlier Chelsea-Derby.

39

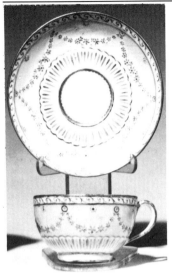

A Royal Crown Derby dessert service, with false gadroon foliate borders in pale and dark pink and gilding, comprising: 5 dishes on pedestal scroll feet and 12 plates, printed marks in black, impressed DERBY, 20th C. **£620-720**

A Derby yellow ground teacup and saucer, moulded with pink swags of flowerheads within an S-scroll pattern rim, crack to base of cup, puce crown, crossed batons and D mark, Wm. Duesbury & Co., c. 1785. **£200-250**

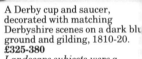

A Derby cup and saucer, decorated with matching Derbyshire scenes on a dark blue ground and gilding, 1810-20. **£325-380**
Landscape subjects were a common theme at Derby. Notable artists were Boreman, Hill, Robertson, Brewer and Lucas.

A Crown Derby teacup and saucer, with pink ground, the cup painted by George Robertson with a frigate flying the Red Ensign, the saucer with other shipping of the Royal Navy, in gilt-framed square panels, puce mark crown, crossed batons and D and pattern no. 447. **£1,300-£1,500**

A pair of Derby heart-shaped dishes, each painted in the manner of Dodson, both within gilt acanthus borders on a duck egg blue ground, 10 in., crown, crossed batons and 'D' mark in red. **£200-300**

A Derby blue-ground topographical part dessert service, painted in the manner of Lucas with named views, 25 pieces, damaged, crown, crossed batons and D marks in iron-red, Robert Bloor & Co., c. 1820. **£2,300-2,600**

A pair of Derby botanical dishes, finely painted in colours with specimen flowers named at the reverse, one with Blue Thomea or Morning Glory, the other with Auricula, within shaped gilt rims, iron-red crown, crossed batons, dot and D marks, c. 1820, 28 cm. wide. **£300-400**

A Crown Derby part dessert service, each piece superbly painted, comprising 4 shell-shape dishes, 2 lobed oval dishes and 2 lobed diamond-shape dishes, named in script and crown, crossed batons and D marks and nos. 3 to 12 in red. **£600-800**

A pair of Royal Crown Derby ewers, painted in colours with heart-shaped panels of roses by Desiré Leroy, one signed, 15.5 cm., printed marks. **£380-480**

A Derby figure of a brindled pug, height 60 cm., late 18th C. **£120-£200**

A pair of Derby figures of red squirrels, c. 1825, 16.5 cm. high. **£700-800**

A Derby group of a cow and reclining calf, on green base with applied flowers, 6½ in., numerals 27 and 10 in red, slight restoration. **£100-150**

A Derby figure of a pedlar, wearing an iron-red and turquoise cape, yellow-lined pink dress and flowered skirt, neck and dress restored, some minor chips and restorations, Wm. Duesbury & Co., c. 1765, 19 cm. high. **£350-400**

A Derby grazing sheep, c. 1765. **£200-300**

A Derby figure of a Scotsman, wearing a blue cap and yellow-lined tartan jacket and breeches, in turquoise cape, white shirt and yellow shoes, head repaired, Wm. Duesbury & Co., c. 1756, 16.5 cm. high. **£350-450**

A pair of Derby white dry-edge figures of a shepherd and shepherdess, hats damaged, his left leg cracked, chips to coat and fingers, she with chips to cuffs and lamb's ear, Andrew Planché period, c. 1753, 17 cm. and 18 cm. high. **£500-600**

A pair of Derby figures of a monk and nun reading books, the pages inscribed 'Spes mea in Deo' and 'Omnia Gloria', chipped and restored W. Duesbury & Co., c. 1770, 14.5 cm. and 13.5 cm. high. **£400-500**

A Derby figure of a girl, wearing a pink bodice, on a base enriched in green, Wm. Duesbury & Co., c. 1760, 23.5 cm. high. **£250-300**

A set of four Derby figures of the Continents, minor chips, Europe repair to her left arm, right hand, crown and cloak, all about 23 cm. high, patch marks, c. 1765. **£1,200-1,800**

Derby figure of a girl, wearing brightly coloured attire, damaged, 6¼ in., and another of a lady gazing into a mirror, ¼ in., the latter with swords mark in blue, late 18th C., both lightly rubbed. **£200-300**

A Bloor Derby figure, with rare mark, 6 in. wide, with damage to bocage: **£110-140.** Perfect: **£175-£200**

A pair of Derby biscuit groups depicting the Elements, 9¼ in., incised N48, c. 1795, one figure with repaired foot, slight chipping **£250-300**
Derby pioneered biscuit porcelain figures in the later years of the 18th C.

43

A Derby figure of Minerva, base chipped, one finger chipped, 13¾ in., c. 1765. **£200-250**

A Derby figure, c. 1775, 8½ in. high. **£500-600**

A Derby figure of shepherd girl, pre Chelsea-Derby, c. 1765, unusual peacock motif on dress, 8 in. high. **£250-320**

A Derby figure of Brittania, c. 1770, 13½ in. high. **£450-550**

A large Derby figure of Sir James Quin as Sir John Falstaff, turquoise breeches, iron-red and gilt jerkin, blade replaced, 20¼ in., incised number 271, early 19th C. **£300-400**

A pair of Derby figures of children, c. 1830-40, marked Bloor Derby, 5½ in high. **£260-£285** pair

A pair of Stevenson Hancock Derby figures, 'The Gardeners', 5 in. high, c. 1862. **£185-200** pair

rare Derby figure of apoleon, c. 1840, 8½ ., slight chip to base. 400-450

A Bloor Derby figure, inscribed 'Prodigious' marked, c. 1825, 6¾ in. high. **£160-185**

A Derby figure of Falstaff, in plumed hat, yellow lined gilt-flowered blue jacket, gilt flowered waistcoat, maroon breeches and brown boots with a gilt sword and shield, sword a replacement, lacks sheath, incised No. 291, script Bloor Derby mark beneath a crown, Robert Bloor & Co., c. 1825, 23 cm. high. **£170-200**

A Derby group of a boy with his spaniel, 6 in., patch marks and ncised No. '49', slight estoration. **£100-150**

A pair of Derby Mansion House dwarfs, one wears a hat advertising an auction, the other a conical shaped hat with a Theatre Royal Haymarket play bill, height 16.8 cm., printed mark, c. 1890. **£280-350**

A pair of Derby ice pails, covers and liners from the Animal Service, painted by John Brewer 1795-1800, 25 cm. high. **£900-£1,100**

45

A Derby inkwell, painted with blue, iron-red and gilt scrolling foliage, iron-red crown, crossed batons and D. mark, Robert Bloor & Co., c. 1820, 10 cm. high. **£250-300**

A Derby mask jug, painted with sprays of coloured flowers, brown edged rim, small chip to spout, 7½ in., c. 1765-70. **£200- £250**
A typical Derby mask jug, the spout moulded as a contemporary man with a tricorn hat, as opposed to the Worcester/ Caughley examples using the classical satyrs mask. Note also the distinctive splayed foot.

A Derby milk jug, with two gilt cartouches containing crests against a yellow ground, crown, crossed batons and D mark in puce, Duesbury & Kean, 15.5 cm. wide, c. 1800. **£550-700**

A large Derby mug, painted in the manner of Moses Webster, 12.8 cm., red enamelled crown over crossed batons mark and number '37', c. 1820. **£300-400**

A Derby mug modelled as the head of Neptune, (slight crack to rim), crown, crossed batons and D mark in iron-red, c. 1810, 12 cm. wide. **£150-200**
Chinese potters successfully copied this jug and exported it back to Europe and America.

One of a pair of Derby plates, painted with exotic birds, slight rim chips, red anchor marks, Wm. Duesbury & Co., about 20.5 cm. diam., c. 1758. **£450-550** the pair.
There is a close resemblance between this plate and Chelsea gold anchor examples painted in the atelier of James Giles.

A Derby cylindrical mug, with looped strap handle, c. 1760, 13 cm. high. **£550-600**

A Derby plate, by Zachariah Boreman, view near Mosley Moor, c. 1782-1800, 8½ in. wide. **£500-600**

A Derby plate, painted with a scene of Lake of Albano, Italy, on a lime green ground, 8½ in. **£300-350**

A Derby armorial plate, reserved on a turquoise scale-pattern, the border gilt with a crest above surmounted by the motto 'Through' crown, crossed batons and D mark in puce, impressed Z, Wm. Duesbury & Co., c. 1790, 23 cm. diam. **£500-700**

A Derby botanical plate, painted with a specimen of Amaryllis Reticulata, 9¼ in., named in blue and crowned batons and D mark and pattern No. 115 in blue. **£100-150**

A Derby botanical deep plate, in the style of 'Quaker' Pegg, outlined with gilt, 10¼ in., named in blue and with crowned batons, and D mark and pattern No. 216 in blue. **£150-200**

A Derby plate, with Swiss landscape, c. 1810-1820, 9 in. wide. **£200-300**

A Derby plate, painted by Moses Webster, 1821-25, 9 in. diam. **£100-140**

A Derby plate with an Italian scene, c. 1820, 9 in. wide. **£250-£300**

A Derby helmet shaped sauceboat, with shell moulded sides, the ribs picked out in underglaze blue, the rim with a flower and trellis pattern border, height 8.5 cm., c. 1760. **£150-180** *Derby produced little blue and white porcelain, but the majority of the output was confined to cream jugs like the present example.*

A Pair of Royal Crown Derby rectangular plaques, painted by C. E. Flowerdew, signed and dated 1882, the reverses with iron-red marks, 42 cm. by 57 cm. **£500-£800**

A Derby blue and white oval
sauceboat, slight crack to base
and handle, Wm. Duesbury &
Co., c. 1768. **£150-200**

An early Derby creamboat,
painted by the 'Cotton stem
painter' with flower sprays and
sprigs, brown edged rim, 4½ in.,
c. 1760-65, slight rubbing. **£200-
£250**
*Note the somewhat academic
flower painting style which is
borrowed from Meissen.*

A rare yellow ground Derby
teapot stand, c. 1790, with puce
mark, 5¼ in. wide. **£165-185**

A Derby scent bottle, with hand
painted flowers on a sky blue
ground, c. 1810-20, 5¼ in. high.
£150-200

An early Derby tureen and
cover, patch marks, cover
cracked, 21 cm. wide, 21 cm.
high, c. 1758-60. **£150-200**

A Royal Crown Derby vase and
cover, painted and signed on
each side by J. Platt, reserved on
a striped gilt-ground between
blue and gilt borders, 16¼ in.,
printed mark in gilding,
c. 1880. **£300-400**

DATING HINTS

- treat 18th C. marks with suspicion until confirmed by study of the porcelain body and glaze but 19th C. marks are *on the whole* reliable (with notable exceptions such as Rockingham)
- it used to be the case that fakers would only direct their art towards the earlier more valuable pieces but as even very recent pieces escalate in value it becomes more tempting (and easier) to fake them. (One only has to think of the recent Bernard Leach pottery fakes to realise the large sums of money to be had by skillful fakery — these also show that 'experts can be duped as easily as the novice collector)
- from 1891 porcelain should bear the mark of the country of origin, eg. 'ENGLAND', 'GERMANY', 'JAPAN' etc.
- from c. 1910 should display 'MADE IN ENGLAND', 'MADE IN GERMANY', 'MADE IN JAPAN', etc.

A pair of Derby eel-basket vases, gold anchor marks, c. 1765, 24 cm. high. **£500-800**

A pair of Royal Crown Derby campana shaped vases, decorated with the Old Crown Derby Witches pattern, height 15 cm., printed mark and date code for 1911. **£200-300**
Derby is particularly noted for its Imari patterns and there is frequent confusion between it and other factories utilising the red, blue and gilt Imari palette.

A pair of Royal Crown Derby vases and covers, painted by C. Harris, on a royal blue ground, signed, one vase and both covers damaged, 7¼ in., printed crowned initials mark, painted pattern number 7773/1506, indistinct date code possibly for 1909. **£300-500**

A pair of Royal Crown Derby vases, in gold on a deep red ground, 15.5 cm., painted mark and date code for 1890. **£210-260**

A pair of Derby crested campana vases, painted by Thomas Steel against a green ground, printed Crowned circle mark, Robert Bloor & Co., 29 cm., high, c. 1830. **£2,700-3,000**

A Royal Doulton figure 'Pantalettes', H.N. 362, 8 in., 1933. **£300-350**

A Royal Doulton figure 'A Victorian Lady', H.N. 728, 7¾ in., 1934. **£120-170**

A Royal Crown Derby vase and cover, the neck restored, printed crowned initials, date code for 1896, 14 in. **£180-240**

A Royal Doulton figure 'Veronica', H.N. 1517, 8 in., 1935. **£300-350**

Left
A Doulton figure of a jester, 9½ in., inscribed marks including C. J. Noke, the title and H.N. 1295, all in iron-red, green printed mark, impressed date 4.10.28. 1928. **£200-250**

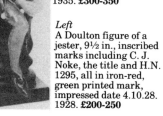

Left
A Royal Doulton figure 'Biddy', H.N. 1445, 5½ in., 1931. **£130-£150**

51

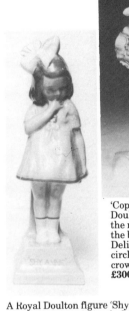

'Coppelia'. A Royal Doulton figure, based on the mechanical doll in the ballet Coppelia by Delibes, 18.5 cm. high, circle mark, lion and crown, H.N. 2115. **£200-£300**

A Royal Doulton figure 'Shy Anne', H.N. 65, 7¾ in., before 1927. **£550-600**

'A Victorian Lady'. A Royal Doulton figure, in green and purple plume, 20.50 cm. high, circle mark, lion and crown, H.N. 1452. **£190-250**

A Royal Doulton vase, painted by Hancock, signed, damaged, printed lion, crown and circle mark, incised shape number, painted pattern number, 14½ in. c. 1910. **£200-300**

A pair of Royal Doulton vases, painted by N. W. Keates, signed, printed lion, crown and circle mark, painted Ra7178E, incised shape number and impressed date code for 1915, 20 cm. **£300-£380**

A fine Royal Doulton cabinet plate, painted by G. White, signed, after Dicksee, with 'Juliet', decorated in raised gilding and bright blue and turquoise enamels, 22.2 cm., printed crowned circular mark, painted title, numbered RA 3970, gilder's initials and impressed date code for 1903. **£400-500**

A pair of Royal Doulton vases, painted by J. Hancock, signed, coloured in tones of sepia on the pale green ground, one restored, 8⅛ in., printed lion, crown and circle, incised shape number 854, c. 1910. **£200-300**

A model of the Goss oven, with slate coloured roof, 7.5 cm., very slight chip to chimney. **£80-120**. If perfect: **£150-175**

The Old Smithy, Gullane, a rare model, red, beige and black, 7.2 cm., printed goshawk and title, early 20th C., minor chip. **£200-250**. If perfect: **£400-500**

A Goss model of Feathers Hotel, Ledbury, black printed title and goshawk, 114 mm. length, chimney missing: **£100-140**. If perfect: **£550-650**

(l.) A Goss cottage, 'Rt. Hon. O. Lloyd George's early home', width 6 cm., glazed. **£100-120**

(r.) A Goss cottage, 'St. Nicholas Chapel, Lantern Hill, Ilfracombe', 7.2 cm. **£80-100**

A Goss Shetland pony, cream-glazed, the base bearing the arms of Chagford, 4¼ in., printed goshawk. **£120-150**

LIVERPOOL

Much discussion has taken place over the last few years as to how many factories in Liverpool were actually producing porcelain in the 18th Century. It has also been assumed that three factories Chaffers, Christian's and Penningtons were the most influential from c. 1754 — the end of the century. Recent research would indicate that there may have been more than one Pennington factory. The accepted dates for the factories:—

- Richard Chaffers & Co.
  c. 1754-1765
- Samuel Gilbody   c. 1754-1761
- William Ball   c. 1755-1769
- William Reid & Co.   c. 1756-1761
- Philip Christian & Co.
  c. 1765-1776
- Seth Pennington   c. 1770-1799
- Wolfe & Co.   c. 1795-1800
  Some points on the different factories

- *Chaffers & Co.* — produced first a bone ash and later a soapstone porcelain, mainly blue and white ware, much good painting, some polychrome wares are of very high quality

- *Samuel Gilbody.* — rarest of Liverpool porcelains, with soft glaze colours tend to sink into glaze; very difficult factory to correctly attribute wares

- *William Ball.* — blue and white slightly more common from this factory, decoration very Bow-like, glaze can be confused with Longton Hall

- *William Reid & Co.* — mainly blue and white specimens, quite crude in appearance, often sanded, chinoiserie based decoration

- *Philip Christian & Co.* — underglaze blue tends to be of a greyish tone: some fine painting; flatware is rare but bowls were something of a speciality

- *Seth Pennington.* — large amount of copies of Christian's wares, standard never reached earlier factories, mainly blue and white wares

- *Wolfe & Co.* — polychrome wares normally use chinoiserie decoration, blue and white wares very rare

A rare blue and white Christian's Liverpool bowl, c. 1765. **£200-250**

A Christian's Liverpool small dish, c. 1765, small chip. **£40-45**. Perfect: **£60-80**

A Chaffer's Liverpool small plate, after a Kang H'si original, painted in underglaze blue with the 'Jumping Boy' pattern, pseudo Chinese mark, 12 cm., c. 1708. **£300-400**
All the Liverpool factories made extensive use of Chinoiserie subjects. This, however, is a straight copy of a Chinese design of the late 17th C.

A Liverpool blue and white fluted sauceboat, lip chips, William Ball's factory, c. 1760. **£240-300**

A Chaffer's Liverpool mug, c. 1760, 3¾ in. high. **£195-215**

A Chaffer's Liverpool bowl, painted in clear 'famille-rose' enamels, 7½ in., c. 1758-62. **£200-300**

A Liverpool small mug, c. 1775, perhaps Pennington's factory, 3¾ in., printed with quail pattern. **£50-60**

A Chaffer's Liverpool blue and white saucer, 4¾ in. diam., c. 1760. **£70-80**

A Liverpool blue and white teabowl and saucer, painted with 'Fisherman' pattern, with printed border, c. 1780. **£40-45**
This pattern is also known at Worcester and Caughley.

A rare William Reid Liverpool tea caddy and cover, in the form of a boy's head, painted with washes of underglaze-blue, 13 cm. **£1,000-1,300**
Most Liverpool products were fairly functional in form. Figures, whether decorative or functional, are exceptionally rare.

LIVERPOOL   LONGTON HALL

A Chaffer's Liverpool blue and
white teabowl and saucer, with
the 'Jumping Boy' pattern,
c. 1758. **£180-220**

A Pennington Liverpool teapot
and cover, with flower
decorations and a 'wet' blue
border, c. 1780. **£100-130**

A pair of Liverpool blue
and white teabowls and
saucers, enriched in
overglaze iron-red and
gold, William Ball's
factory, c. 1760. **£300-£350**

A Wolfe's Liverpool teabowl and
saucer, with typical Chinoiserie
pink decoration, c. 1780. **£60-90**

A Liverpool teapot and cover,
moulded and painted in enamel
colours on a cream coloured
ground, with an iron-red foliate
border, height 15 cm., late
18th C., cover damaged. **£100-£150**

A Longton Hall cabbage-leaf
moulded bowl, the centre painted
by 'The Castle Painter', minute
rim chips, crack to base, c. 1755
21.5 cm. diam. **£1,000-1,200**
*Vegetable forms were particularly
popular at Longton Hall.*

56

LONGTON HALL

- factory founded by William Jenkinson in c. 1749
- in 1751 he was joined by Wm. Littler and Wm. Nicklin
- earliest pieces the 'Snowman' figures and some blue and white wares
- painting tends to have a primitive, slightly crude look
- the figures, in particular, tend to have a stiff appearance
- the porcelain is of the glassy soft-paste type
- the glaze can tend to have a greenish/grey appearance
- pieces often thickly potted
- Duesbury worked at Longton Hall before going to Derby
- the 'middle period' of the factory from c. 1754-1757 saw the best quality porcelain produced
- much of the output of the middle period was moulded
- two famous painters from the period are the 'Castle painter' and the 'trembly rose' painter
- Sadler's black printed wares are extremely rare and sought after
- the porcelain is generally unmarked
- if marked it is usually 2 crossed L's with dots below
- very similar in some ways to Plymouth it is thought that Longton Hall moulds were sold to Cookworthy
- the factory closed in 1760 — all wares are now rare

A Longton Hall candlestick group of two putti in a pale lemon puce robe, on a circular pad base, applied with pink, blue and yellow flowers and green trailing foliage, damage to left arm, dolphin lacks tail, repair to nozzle, c. 1755, 21.5 cm. high overall. **£300-400**

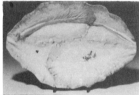

A Longton Hall leaf-moulded dish, painted with a flower spray and an insect, the underside with a firing crack disguised by a green leaf, c. 1755, 30.5 cm. wide. **£350-450**

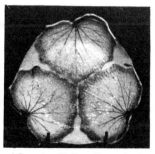

A Longton Hall mulberry leaf dish, with typical Longton Hall moulding and decoration, c. 1758. **£300-400**

A pair of English porcelain figures of seated pugs, both tails restored, one forepaw repaired and one with crack to neck, Longton Hall or Lowestoft, 18th C., 9 cm. high. **£500-550**

LONGTON HALL

A Longton Hall figure of Winter, slight chips, c. 1755, 12 cm. high. **£350-400**

A Longton Hall mug, with 'pecking parrot' decoration, decorated by Littler in this typical Westpans manner. **£450-£500**

A rare Longton Hall spoon tray, c. 1753-57. **£500-600**

A Longton Hall vase and cover, painted with exotic birds enclosed by cartouches, with flower encrusted lid and lime green band around the foot, 21 cm., mid 18th C., damaged. **£100-150**
Note the somewhat clumsy appearance typical of many of the Longton Hall forms.

A Longton Hall two-handled vase and cover, painted in colours with exotic birds in landscape vignettes, part of base repaired, chips to flowerheads and foliage, the cover leaning to one side, 43 cm. high, c. 1755. **£1,000-1,300**

A Lowestoft coffee cup and saucer, c. 1772. **£60-100**

A pair of Lowestoft baskets, printed in underglaze-blue with the 'pine-cone' pattern, 9¼ in., c.1775-85. **£370-450**
Similar baskets were made at Worcester.

A Lowestoft polychrome bowl, c. 1790, 4 in. diam. **£80-100**

A Lowestoft blue and white inscribed and dated cylindrical inkwell, the side with the inscription 'P. High/Lowestoft/ 1798', the reverse with a trailing flowering branch, 7 cm. diam. **£1,000-1,300**
Lowestoft produced numerous inscribed or commemorative pieces.

A Lowestoft blue and white pickle dish, c. 1770. **£65-75**
Similar pickle dishes were manufactured at Bow.

A Lowestoft blue and white patty pan, with painted butterfly, no glaze inside, 3⅜ in. diam., c. 1770. **£70-90**

A Lowestoft plate, painted in underglaze-blue with a female Oriental figure, blue painter's number '3' inside footrim, 22 cm., c. 1765-70, small crack and chip. **£350-430**

A Lowestoft plate, painted in underglaze-blue with a female Oriental figure, 22.9 cm., blue painter's mark '5' inside footrim, about 1765-70, scratched and stained, minute rim chips. **£250-£350**

This plate is inscribed with the numeral '5', associated with Robert Allen.

A Lowestoft plate, painted in underglaze-blue with an Oriental fisherman, blue painter's numeral '3' inside footrim, 23 cm., c. 1765-70, minute rim chips, slight scratching and staining. **£300-£400**

Painter's numeral 3 is usually associated with Richard Phillips

A Lowestoft blue and white fluted oval stand, painter's number '8', c. 1762, 18.5 cm. wide. **£250-300**

A Lowestoft tea caddy and cover moulded with flowers and leaves around four panels, painted in inky blue colours with an Oriental landscape, height 9.2 cm., late 18th C. **£200-250**

A Lowestoft teapot and cover of rare barrel shape, with open flower finial, painted in colour in Chinese style, the reverse with a Chinaman on an island, red loop and dot border, 4¾ in. **£500-700**

A Lowestoft sparrow-beak cream jug, 3⅜ in. **£150-200**

A rare Lowestoft polychrome butter pot or small tureen and cover, moulded with fine vertical flutes, painted in colours, 13 cm., restored. **£400-500**

A Minton's moon flask and stand, traced in red on the richly gilded body, height 33 cm., impressed mark and retailer's mark, late 19th C., cover missing, some damage. **£80-120**

MINTON

- factory site bought in 1793 by Thomas Minton at Stoke on Trent
- Minton had worked at Caughley and Spode
- factory first produced earthenware, started to make porcelain c. 1798
- factory mainly famous for its bone china
- early patterns tend to be very similar to Newhall, Pinxton and Spode
- early wares not marked but did often have a pattern number, sometimes with N. or No. in front
- Minton palette is closest to Pinxton
- much pre 1850 Minton is wrongly ascribed to other factories, particularly Rockingham, Coalport and Pinxton
- some collectors have switched from Swansea and Nantgarw having realised the quality of Minton. Much of Mintons flower painting is unsurpassed
- the early figures are prone to damage — watch for restoration
- very little heavily flower encrusted wares have escaped without damage
- some beautiful ground colours with excellent gilding, Minton had particular success with a turquoise ground
- as with most other factories, signed pieces are most desirable
- artists of note include:– G. Hancock, J. Bancroft, T. Kirkby, T. Allen, R. Pilsbury, Jesse Smith and A. Boullemier
- note marks:– MINTON became MINTONS from c. 1873

A Mintons pate-sur-pate circular dish, decorated by Louis Marc Solon in white slip on an olive green ground, inscribed on the reverse 'The Bacchanalian Muse', the rim gilt, signed, gilt Mintons and retailer's mark for Phillips, Oxford Street, London, 23.5 cm. diam. **£400-600**

MINTON

MINTONS PATE-SUR-PATE

This technique was devised at Sevres in the 1860's in an attempt to emulate the Chinese. The term means 'paste on paste' and achieved an effect very like a porcelain cameo. The artist started with a coloured parian base onto which he built up layers of slip, which he then carved. Once this was fired, the white slip became variably translucent, allowing tones of the darker colour underneath to show through. It was a difficult technique and one which depended greatly on the skill of the craftsman who was dealing, prior to firing, with opaque material. The main exponent of the technique at Minton was M. L. Solon who arrived at Minton from Sevres in 1870. His signed pieces command high prices. His pupils, include his son Leon, Alboine and Lawrence Birks, H. Hollins and T. Mellor. Alboine Birks in particular could on occasion rival his teachers work, certainly in terms of his flowers and foliage

A Minton plate, with typical bright turquoise ground and jewelled gilding, c. 1860. **£200-£250**

A pair of Minton 'Cloisonne' moon flasks, with a turquoise ground, hair cracks, 32.1 cm., impressed Mintons, 166, indistinct date code, c. 1870. **£500-600**

A Mintons pate-sur-pate moon flask, deep olive green body decorated in white, 25.4 cm., impressed and printed marks, moulded shape number, c. 1900. **£300-400**

A Minton blue and white coffee can and saucer, c. 1810. **£30-35**

A Minton part dessert service, comprising: 4 comports and 12 plates, impressed mark, and cypher for 1863, two plates and one comport damaged. **£200-300**

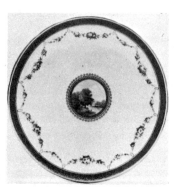

A Minton plate, with turquoise border and gilt rim, 9 in., c. 1865. **£60-70**

A Minton plate, with puce cupid, possibly by T. Kirkby, c. 1870, 10 in. wide. **£50-60**

A Boullemier Minton plate, with pierced border and gilt jewelling, c. 1885, restored: **£300-340.** Perfect: **£500-550**

A Minton circular plaque, painted by J. E. Dean, signed, 9⅜ in., late 19th C. **£250-£300**

A Minton 'globe pot pourri' vase and cover, painted with a view of an Elizabethan country house, bordered cartouche inscribed in puce 'Guy's Cliff', the reverse with a large bouquet of summer flowers, 19.5 cm., c. 1825-30, chipped. **£200-300**
Much of the early Minton flower-encrusted porcelain pieces, such as the above example, were for many years thought to have been the products of the Coalport/ Coalbrookedale concern.

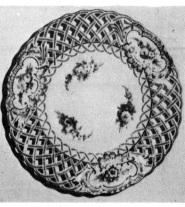

A Minton plate, with pierced border, impressed mark, small piece of enamelling missing, c. 1890. **£65-75.** Perfect: **£100+**

A Minton pot pourri vase
(gondole), in the Sevres style,
minor chips to finial, 27 cm.
high. **£800-1,000**
*Minton made numerous copies of
Sevres porcelain in the 1860's
and 70's. Some pieces occasionally
appear in catalogues as French.*

A pair of rare Minton 'Dresden
scroll' vases and covers, painted
with panels of summer flowers
and a pastoral scene, coloured in
pastel shades. **£600-800**

A pair of Minton vases and
covers, reserved on a bright-blue
ground, chips, knops restored,
16½ in., rare
printed belt mark and crown,
affixed paper label for T. Goode
& Co., c. 1860. **£500-700**

A Minton vase and cover,
painted with nude figures of
Venus and Diana, against a
turquoise ground, the reverse
with musical trophies, printed
mark, 33 cm. high. **£200-250**

A pair of Minton pate-sur-pate
porcelain vases, 12½ in. **£400-
£500**

A rare Newhall presentation jug,
well painted in colours, the front
with gilt monogram TG within a
wreath, 19 cm. **£450-550**

NEWHALL

- Newhall was the second Staffordshire pottery to sucessfully make porcelain, Longton Hall being the first (although Neale may have been making porcelain)

- the usual date for the commencement of the factory is 1782, however, then it was known as Hollins, Warburton & Company

- porcelain is a greyish colour to transmitted light and is seldom crazed

- Duvivier, who had worked at Derby and Worcester, also painted at Newhall from 1782-1790 — because of the rarity of attributable pieces one wonders if some of his work at Newhall has been wrongly attributed to another factory

- very few pre-1790 wares had a pattern number

- around 1812 a new bone-china body was introduced and the factory was by this time known as Newhall

- after 1820 the bone-china wares seemed to lose some quality and the factory closed in 1835

- Newhall, above all other 18th C. English factories, has seen what can only be called an explosion in price in the last year. This has probably been caused by the disparaging attitude of many porcelain dealers to the more ordinary Newhall wares in the past and hence their underpricing

A Newhall cream jug, pattern 195, c. 1790-1805, 4½ in. high. **£60- 70**

A Newhall waisted rectangular dessert plate, the centre printed in bright enamel colours, within a border moulded on a light blue ground, all heightened with gold, 23.5 cm., early 19th C., printed New Hall mark, pattern No. 1478. **£100-140**

A Newhall pale blue ground part dessert service, the centres printed and coloured with fruit with gilt foliage, the borders moulded in white relief, comprising: a rectangular centre dish, sauce tureens, covers and fixed stands, 2 oval dishes (one cracked), 2 rectangular dishes, 4 shell dishes and 18 plates (one cracked), pattern No. 1706, c. 1815. **£600-700**

A Newhall fluted plate, in the manner of Duvivier, sparsely painted, within a pink border with gilt and grey-green medallions, c. 1785, 21 cm. diam. **£200-250**

A Newhall hard paste tea bowl
and saucer, pattern No. 421,
c. 1790. **£40-45**

A Newhall hard paste tea bowl
and saucer, pattern No. 191,
c. 1790. **£40-45**

A Newhall teacup and saucer,
pattern 446, 1795-1810, with
workman's mark. **£45-52**
*This shaped cup, the so-called
'Bute', was generally adopted by
all English factories in the early
years of the 19th C.*

A Newhall trio, pattern 1153,
c. 1810. **£40-50**

A Newhall cup and saucer,
pattern No. 1677, c. 1815. **£35-40**
*The London shaped cups, like the
ovoid 'Bute' form, were produced
by nearly all English factories in
the early 19th C.*

A Newhall cup, pattern 186. **£20-
£25**
*The decoration on this cup is
based on a 'Compagnie des Indes'
design.*

A rare Newhall 'named view' tea and coffee service, bat printed in black and picked out in coloured enamels with landscape vignettes, some named beneath, including 'Winstone Cottage, Brecknock', 'Newham Court', 'Twickenham Meadows', comprising: teapot and cover, milk jug, sucrier and cover, 2 saucer dishes, slop bowl, 10 teacups, 4 coffee cans, and 12 saucers, pattern No. 984 in yellow, iron-red and sepia enamels, c. 1815, some damage. £400-600

A Newhall teapot and cover, pattern No. 421, spout restored, c. 1785, 5½ in. £60-80

A Newhall 70 piece part tea and coffee service, painted in an Imari palette with the 'Tobacco Leaf' pattern, damaged, pattern No. 274, c. 1800. £1,400-1,600

PINXTON

A Newhall teapot and stand, pattern 425. £185-200
The mandarin designs were copied from contemporary Chinese export ware.

- Billingsley persuaded John Coke to set up a factory at Pinxton which commenced c. 1796
- Billingsley left in 1799
- in the early stages the porcelain, glaze and even designs are very similar to Derby
- the body has good translucency
- in comparison with other factories the palette has a yellow/brown look
- the glaze is of a fine 'creamy' white with the occasional slight suggestion of blue
- the enamels tend to have subdued or pastel tones
- well known for its excellent flower painting (some no doubt by Billingsley) and also local landscape painting
- the factory closed in 1812/13 but it is not certain how much porcelain was produced from 1805 to the closure
- Pinxton is a rare factory and the yellow ground wares, in particular, are highly sought after

A Pinxton beaker, the side painted with figures by castle ruin, reserved on a yellow ground, 3⅛ in., c. 1800. £400-£500
Yellow is a popular ground colour on Pinxton.

67

A Pinxton yellow ground D-shaped crocus pot and pierced cover, painted in a pale palette with a mountainous wooded landscape, flanked by two yellow panels, minute chip to rim at back, c. 1800, 17.5 cm. wide. **£1,800- 2,500**

D-shaped bulb or bough pots were produced at many early 19th C. factories. The scrolled base is unique to Pinxton.

PLYMOUTH

- factory ran from c. 1768-1772
- a hard-paste porcelain body patented by William Cookworthy
- high proportion of kiln wastage
- had a tendancy to staining and many imperfections in the glaze
- resembled Bow and Longton Hall
- decoration often Chinese 'famille verte' or 'Mandarin' style
- very blackish underglaze blue
- Cookworthy transferred the factory to Bristol c. 1771

A pair of Pinxton pale salmon-pink flower pots and stands, with gilt ring handles, painted in the manner of William Billingsley with 'Papplewick Hall, Notts.', some minor rubbing to gilding, c. 1800, 12.5 cm. wide. **£2,000 - £3,000**

A Plymouth mug, painted with a garden landscape scene in underglaze blue, 16.2 cm., marked with the symbol for tin, restoration to foot, c. 1770. **£100-£150**

The bell-shaped tankard with a splayed foot was popular at Plymouth. Collectors should beware of French hard-paste copies.

A Plymouth sweetmeat, in the white, some restoration, height 15.5 cm., c. 1770. **£200-250**

A Plymouth baluster mug, with an iron-red loop-and-dot pattern rim, c. 1770, 15.5 cm. high. **£1,600-1,650**

RIDGWAY

- one of the most important factories manufacturing English bone china
- most of the early Ridgway porcelain from 1808-1830 is unmarked; some however do have pattern numbers which are fractional
- the quality of the early porcelain is excellent, brilliant white and with no crazing in the glaze
- in 1830 the partnership between John and William Ridgway was dissolved; John continued to produce quality porcelain
- there were many skilled flower painters employed at the Cauldon Place works including George Hancock, Thomas Brentnall, Joseph Bancroft
- the development of the Ridgway factory is as follows:– John Ridgway & Company 1830-1855, John Ridgway, Bates & Company 1856-1858, Bates, Brown-Westhead & Moore 1859-1861, Brown-Westhead, Moore & Company 1862-1905, Cauldon Ltd. 1906-1920, Cauldon Potteries Ltd 1920-1962

A Ridgway sucrier and cover, 7 in. high, c. 1850. **£35-40**

A flared cylindrical Rockingham pot pourri basket and pierced cover, in pink and yellow, minute chipping to flowers, chip to underside of rim, puce griffin mark, and CL3 in red, c. 1835, 8.5 cm. diam. **£270-350**

A green-ground leaf-shaped Rockingham chamber candlestick, edged in gilding, puce griffin mark, c. 1835, 12.5 cm. wide. **£280-360**

A Ridgway cup and saucer, c. 1820. **£40-46**

A Staffordshire green-ground dessert service, probably Ridgway, painted with flowers within a green caillouté border and a gilt rim, comprising: 8 plates, 3 oval dishes, 2 square dishes and a fruit stand, some wear and discolouration, plate: 23.7 cm., painted pattern No. 761, c. 1830. **£200-250**

ROCKINGHAM

- **works had for a long time produced pottery**
- **porcelain factory opened c. 1826 and closed in 1842**
- **potters of the Brameld family**
- **bone china appears softer than contemporaries**
- **of a smoky ivory/oatmeal colour**
- **glaze had a tendency to irregular fine crazing**
- **factory known for rococo style of decoration, frequently with excellent quality flower painting**
- **tended to use green, grey and puce**
- **large number of erroneous attributions made to the Rockingham factory, especially pieces actually made at Minton and Coalport**
- **pattern numbers over 2,000 are *not* Rockingham**

A Rockingham figure of John Liston as Madame Vestris, inscribed 'Buy a Broom', neck repaired, red griffin mark and incised No. 6, 1826-30, 16 cm. high. **£800-1,000**

A Rockingham rectangular bombe desk set, painted with bouquets of garden flowers, restored, puce marks and CL4 in iron-red, c. 1835, 23.5 cm. wide. **£500-600**

A miniature Rockingham perrywinkle-blue ground ewer and basin, with gilt twig handle and gilt line rims, the basin with red griffin mark, both pieces with CL2 in red, 1826-30, the ewer 5 cm. high, the basin 6.5 cm. diam. **£370-470**

A Rockingham white figure of a seated hound, impressed Rockingham, Works, Brameld, incised No. 101 and CL1 in red, 1826-30, 7.5 cm. high. **£200-250**

A Rockingham figure of a seated cat, ears chipped, impressed Rockingham Works Brameld, incised No. 77 and 1 size and CL2 in red, 1826-30, 6.5 cm high. **£400-450**

A Rockingham figure of a recumbent ram, with gilt horns, impressed Rockingham Works Brameld, incised No. 109 and CL1 in red, 1826-30, 7 cm. wide. **£360-400**

A pair of Rockingham green-ground oviform jugs, inscribed 'Beagle' and 'Vanish with crack to rim, 'Beagle' with crack to body, raised 7 and puce griffin marks, c. 1835, 13 cm. high. **£380-400** pr.

A Rockingham figure of Paysanne de Sagran en Tirol, minor chips, incised Rockingham Works Brameld and No. 22 and CL2 in red, 1826-30, 18 cm. high. **£500-600**

A Rockingham tea and coffee service, with primrose yellow borders, painted with flowers in pale green and gold, comprising: teapot and cover, sugar basin and cover, milk jug, bowl, 2 cake plates, 12 tea cups, 12 coffee cups and 12 saucers, the saucers with griffin mark in puce and Rockingham Works Brameld Manufacturer to the King, pattern No. 952. **£1,100-1,500** *'Rockingham' has been a much abused term in the past. Almost all neo-rococo services produced in this country were designated 'Rockingham' by auctioneers and dealers alike. The Rockingham glaze is often a pleasant warm cream, almost oatmeal in colour, with an irregular network of crackle.*

A Rockingham rectangular plaque, painted by William W. Bailey, the reverse inscribed in fine red script 'Windsor Castle, from a drawing by P. Dewint, Esqr. W. W. Bailey, Pinx^t, China Works, Wath', 10.5 cm. by 16.3 cm. **£350-450**

Miller's is a price GUIDE Not a price LIST.

The price ranges given reflect the average price a purchaser should pay for similar items. Condition, rarity of design or pattern, size, colour, pedigree, restoration and many other factors must be taken into account when assessing values.

A Rockingham plate, 'To the King' mark, 9 in. wide, c. 1830-37. **£180-220**

A Rockingham plate, painted by Edwin Steele, red mark, c. 1826, 9 in. wide. **£750-820**

A white Rockingham scent bottle and gilt stopper, with gilt line rims, puce griffin mark, and CL1 in gold, c. 1835, 8 cm. high. **£150-200**

A Rockingham figure of Bacchus, with gilding, restoration to chest and head, impressed Rockingham Works Brameld, incised No.30, 1826-30, 15 cm. high. **£350-450**

A Rockingham plate, puce marked, decorated by Bagnley, 9 in. wide, c. 1842. **£330-370**

SPODE

- porcelain was produced from 1790's
- usually credited with the introduction of bone china
- a fine white body
- richly decorated
- felspar porcelain started in 1821
- Copeland and Garrett took over factory in 1833

A Spode coffee can, with gilding, c. 1820. **£32-40**

A Rockingham crested toast-rack, with three pierced gilt foliate racks, gilt with the initial R beneath an earl's coronet, puce griffin mark, c. 1835, 21 cm. wide. **£450-500**

A pair of Spode two-handled pot pourri jars and covers, details in gold, height 10 cm., written mark Spode 2910, early 19th C. **£180-250**

One of a pair of Spode Copeland and Garret plates, replacement for a Chinese armorial service, c. 1833-47, 8 in. diam. **£30-33** pair

A porcelain baluster vase, probably Spode, with gilt scroll and foliage borders and gilt dentil rim, roof repaired, c. 1820, 16.5 cm. high. **£140-180**

A Spode two-handled vase, painted on either side in enamel colours with flowers on a cobalt scale gilded ground, height 31 cm., pattern no. 1166, mid 19th C. **£1,000-1,500**

A Spode pot and cover, pattern 967, c. 1826. **£135-160**

A pair of Wedgwood porcelain plates, with rare red mark, c. 1812-22, 8½ in. diam. **£220-260** pair.
Although a beautiful bone china, it was never a commercial success and its manufacture was abandoned after ten years in 1822.

73

WEDGWOOD FAIRYLAND LUSTRE

- the Wedgwood factory had been experiencing serious financial difficulties during the closing years of the 19th C.
- Daisy Makeig-Jones helped bring about a total reversal with the introduction of her 'Fairyland Lustre'
- the patterns for 'The First Ten Lustre Decorations' Z4823 were published in October 1914
- the butterflies of the First Series tended to be of the 'solid' variety, which were normally printed in gold
- the butterflies of the Second Series were 'open' and were filled with various colours
- in 1917 perhaps the most successful of Daisy's natural lustre subjects — The Hummingbird, was perfected
- the 'Fairy' lustre subjects now command high prices at auction, particularly the more unusual lustre colour combinations

A Wedgwood fairyland lustre bowl, the interior decorated with the 'Jumping Fawn' pattern, the exterior with the 'Woodland Elves III Feather Hat' pattern, diam. 20.5 cm., printed gilt urn mark, painted numerals Z5462 in black, c. 1925. **£500-600**

A Wedgwood flame fairyland lustre bowl, decorated with the 'Running Figures' pattern and the 'Bird in a Hoop' pattern, 21.3 cm., printed urn mark, Z5360, 1920's. **£700-800**

A Wedgwood fairyland lustre bowl, the interior with the 'Feather Hat' variation of the 'Woodland Elves' pattern, the exterior with the 'Poplar Trees' pattern, 24.4 cm., printed urn mark, Z4968, 1920's. **£550-620**

A Wedgwood fairyland lustre plaque, decorated with 'Elves and Spider's Web' pattern Z5288, 27 cm. by 19.5 cm., gilt Portland Vase mark, in gilt frame. **£800-£1,000**

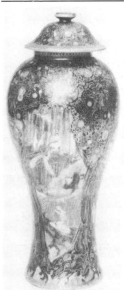

A Wedgwood fairyland lustre vase and cover, decorated with the 'Jewelled Tree' design with 'Copper Trees' and 'Cat and Mouse' panels, 28.5 cm., gilt urn mark, Z4968 incised 2046, 1920's **£900-1,000**

A pair of Wedgwood fairyland lustre vases, decorated with 'Butterfly Women', 15 cm., printed urn mark, Z4968, 1920's **£600-£680**

A Wedgwood fairyland lustre 'Florentine' vase, decorated with the 'Goblins' pattern, 17.5 cm., printed urn mark, incised shape number 3281, 1924-29. **£900-£1,100**

A Wedgwood fairyland lustre vase, decorated with the 'Candlemas' design, the rim and foot with 'Flaming Wheel' borders, 17.6 cm., printed urn mark, Z5157, 1920's. **£380-450**

A Wedgwood fairyland lustre bowl, the interior decorated with the 'Fairy Gondola' pattern, the exterior with a border of 'Flight of Birds' pattern, diam. 32.6 cm., c. 1925. **£500-600**

A pair of Wedgwood fairyland lustre 'Florentine' vases, decorated with the 'Goblins' design in bright colours, 21 cm., gilt urn mark, Z5367, incised 3283, 1924-29. **£1,100-1,300**

A Wedgwood fairyland lustre bowl, decorated with the 'Woodland Elves VIII, Boxing Match' pattern and the 'Castle on a Road' pattern, 28.5 cm., printed urn mark, Z5125, 1920's, wood stand. **£800-900**

WORCESTER PATTERNS

- early period wares mainly confined to chinoiserie decoration
- in the late First Period polychrome wares:–
- most valuable standard type of decoration is birds, particularly if painted by James Giles
- this is followed by English flowers
- then Continental flowers
- and finally the rather stylised Oriental flowers
- it cannot be stressed strongly enough with Worcester that any rim rubbing or wear will greatly reduce the value, often by as much as half

A pair of Worcester oval baskets, printed with the 'Pine Cone' pattern crescent mark in blue, c. 1780. **£500-700**

A Worcester blue-scale pierced circular flared basket, the centre painted with a swag of garden flowers within a shaped gilt scroll cartouche, on a blue-scale ground, blue square seal mark, c. 1770, 24 cm. diam. **£1,600-2,000**

A Worcester blue and white bottle, painter's mark, c. 1758, 26 cm. high. **£450-520**
A fine example of early Worcester blue and white. The designs were 'Chinoiserie', not direct copies of Chinese porcelain.

A Worcester blue and white 'Blue Rock or Cannonball' pattern bowl, 4¾ in. **£60-75**

A Worcester bowl, 'Sampan' pattern, c. 1765, 6 in. wide. **£95-£105**

A Dr. Wall period Worcester bowl, with Chinese 'pagoda' pattern, 9½ in. diam., slight chips to rim. **£130-180.** Perfect: **£300-340**

A rare Dr. Wall bowl, decorated with a portrait of the King of Prussia and a winged figure of Fame, 5 in. wide, c. 1757. **£246-£265**

A Worcester blue and white bowl, the interior decorated with the 'Pine Cone' pattern, the exterior printed with vegetables, butterflies and a snail, width 25.5 cm., crescent mark, c. 1780. **£200-250**

A Barr, Flight & Barr Worcester bowl, on claret ground, 7 in. diam., c. 1810. **£180-190**

An important Worcester armorial punchbowl, the centre painted with the arms of Fry impaling Leigh, and motto Vivons Unis, 28 cm. diam., square mark. **£1,500-2,000** *Made for Rowland Fry Esq. of Banstead, Surrey, who married c. 1770 Bliss Leigh Spencer, daughter of Ann Leigh and Henry Spencer of Thorpe. The armorial incorrectly takes Leigh instead of Spencer as the impalement as the arms of Leigh were probably more established, and the demi-horse crest has been invented for use here and was never granted to Fry, whose arms bear no crest.*

A Flight, Barr & Barr Worcester square salad bowl, from the Stowe service, impressed mark, c. 1813, 27.5 cm. wide. **£1,600-£1,750**

77

A Worcester moulded butter tub, c. 1768, crescent mark, 5¼ in.
£80-90

A Royal Worcester cachepot in Aesthetic Movement taste, chip to foot, 16 cm., incised 604, impressed and printed crowned circle, date code for 1883. **£150-£200**

A Royal Worcester chamberstick, handle damaged, 6 in., 1893.
£90-120

A Grainger's Worcester pierced centrepiece, in turquoise and gilt, black printed marks, 77 cm. high. **£1,000-1,200**

ROYAL WORCESTER

Some Royal Worcester artists and their specialities

C. Baldwyn — birds, particularly swans, George Johnson — exotic birds, James Stinton — game birds, John Stinton — highland cattle, Harry Stinton — highland cattle (more vivid colours than father), R. Rushton — landscapes, R. Sebright — fruit and flowers, H. Price — fruit, J. Stanley — hunting scenes, E. Barker — sheep, Kitty Blake — blackberries and autumnal leaves

A Worcester three shell centrepiece, the fluted shells edged in pink and painted in the manner of James Giles with bouquets of flowers, one shell cracked, another with a firing crack, c. 1768, 16.5 cm. wide. **£450-600** *Shell dishes are comparatively rare at Worcester.*

A Barr, Flight and Barr Worcester coffee can and saucer, painted in bright enamels and gilt, impressed crown BFB monogram. **£45-70**

A Worcester fluted coffee cup and saucer, the border enriched with trellis-pattern and gilt herring-bone pattern, gilt crescent mark, c. 1775. **£500-550**

A Worcester fluted coffee cup and saucer, with 'Prunus Root' pattern, c. 1756-58, with workman's mark. **£240-280**

A Worcester blue and white 'Gilly Flower' cup and saucer. **£115-135**

A Worcester puce-ground coffee cup and saucer, painted in the atelier of James Giles, within gilt line rims, blue crossed swords and 9 mark, c. 1775. **£1,300-1,500**

79

WORCESTER

A Worcester cup and saucer, with gros bleu border, and bird in centre, c. 1765. **£420-490**

A First Period Worcester blue and white coffee cup and saucer, with the 'Fisherman' pattern, c. 1790. **£95-105**
The Fisherman's pattern also appears on Caughley wares.

A Royal Worcester demi-tasse, painted and signed by Harry Stinton, 1924. **£150-165**

A Worcester, Flight, Barr & Barr cabinet cup, on cobalt blue ground, with moth handles, c. 1820. **£200-240**

A pair of Worcester apple-green ground shell-shaped dishes, the centres printed in gilt and green within a sunburst surround, the rims with a similar band in apple-green, enriched in gilt, 19.5 cm. wide, c. 1770.
Along with turquoise, claret and yellow, green is a rare colour as it is difficult to fire successfully. There are many examples of genuine Worcester wares which have been later over-decorated with these colours.

A 1st Period Worcester scalloped dish decorated with the cornflower pattern, c. 1765, script W mark, 7 in. diam. **£150-£165**

A Royal Worcester powder-blue ground part dessert service, painted by H. Martin, with lobed gilt rims, comprising: 2 circular dishes (1 cracked), 2 cushion-shaped dishes, 2 lozenge-shaped dishes (1 cracked), 12 plates, signed, printed marks and pattern No. W9551 X. **£850-£1,100**

A 1st period Worcester gros bleu saucer dish, with English flowers, 7½ in. wide. **£350-400**

A Dr. Wall Worcester dish, pierced and painted with English flowers, dry blue border, c. 1765. **£950-1,050**

A Worcester gros bleu dish, with English flowers, 8½ in. wide. **£265-300**

A Worcester saucer dish, decorated with the Sir Joshua Reynolds pattern, 10 in., c. 1770, perfect: **£785-810.** Rubbed: **£400-£430**

A blue scale Worcester dish, decorated with English flowers, c. 1770, 8¾ in. wide. **£350-400**

A Royal Worcester oval dish, with deep blue and pink grounds, painted by Richard Sebright, signed, 27 cm., date code for 1918. **£250-300**

81

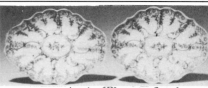

A Worcester blue and white shaped square dish, printed with the 'Pine Cone' pattern, 21 cm. square, blue crescent mark, c. 1765. **£100-150**

A pair of Worcester fluted lozenge-shaped dishes, painted with the 'Earl Manvers Pattern', with berried foliage and puce C-Scrolls from pink diaper-pattern borders enriched with gilt scrolls and green foliage, rubbed, c. 1770, 23.5 cm. wide. **£700-900**

A pair of Worcester, Barr, Flight & Barr cushion shaped dishes, with a circular gilt husk pattern catouche reserved on a marbled grey ground within gilt line rims, one with script mark, both with incised B marks, c. 1805, 25.5 cm. wide. **£440-500**

A Worcester kidney-shaped dish painted with the 'Bengal Tiger' pattern, lightly enriched in gilding, within a gilt line rim, 26.5 cm. wide, and another with slight rim chip, 26 cm. wide, c. 1770. **£260-360** the two

A pair of Worcester, Flight, Barr & Barr cushion-shaped dishes, painted with named views of 'Rhayader Bridge, Radnorshire' and 'Kirkham Priory Gateway, Yorkshire', minute chips to underside of rims, impressed and full script marks, c. 1820, 23 cm. wide. **£200-250**

A Worcester blue and white cress dish, with printed 'Pine Cone' pattern, c. 1770. **£170-190**

A Worcester blue and white painted ewer, decorated with the 'Immortelle' pattern, c. 1780, 5½ in. high. **£195-215**

A pair of Royal Worcester 'New Large Grecian Water-carriers', 52 cm., printed crowned circle mark, shape number 125 and date code for 1912. **£500-550**

A Worcester blue and white shell dish, with bird and workman's mark, c. 1756. **£300-340**

WORCESTER PORCELAIN DATES

1751-1783 *First Period,* **1751-1774** *Dr. Wall Period,* **1776-1793** *Davis/ Flight or Middle Period,* **1793- 1807** *Flight and Barr Period,* **1807- 1813** *Barr, Flight and Barr,* **1813- 1840** *Flight, Barr and Barr,* **1840- 1852** *Chamberlain and Company,* **1852-1862** *Kerr and Binns (W. H. Kerr & Company),* **1862** *Royal Worcester Porcelain Company*

A pair of Grainger & Co. pierced ewers, pierced with lobed panels of flowers amongst foliage, the borders gilt, 22 cm., printed shield mark, painted pattern number 1/1928, c. 1890. **£230- £300**

A rare Royal Worcester figure of a sailor-boy, wearing lilac bell-bottom trousers, orange and pale yellow shirt and green hat, the enamels 'shot' with gilding, 18 cm., printed crowned circle mark, shape number 2012, Rd. No. 3213(?)88, date code for 1898. **£500-800**

A Royal Worcester 'Hadley' fountain group, in a bronzed glaze, height 17.6 cm., printed mark and date code for 1917. **£220-300**

A rare early Worcester finger bowl and stand, painted in underglaze blue with the 'Cormorant' pattern, 7.5 cm. and 15.5 cm., both with workman's mark resembling a musical note, c. 1756. **£1,000-£1,200**

A Royal Worcester figure of John Bull, hat brim damaged, signed Hadley on pillar, green printed mark, impressed marks, 1898, 6¾ in. **£90-140**

A rare Royal Worcester figure of a puritan, glazed overall in creamy white with gilt details and printed scattered flowers, 18 cm., impressed and printed crowned circle, date code for 1918. **£120-180**

A Worcester scroll-moulded bombe flowerpot, the sides with 3 foliage-moulded cartouches, enriched in puce and painted with birds in flight, c. 1758, 22 cm. wide. **£2,400-3,000**
A good example of English rococo.

A Worcester blue and white stand for a finger bowl, rim chipped, painter's mark, c. 1755, 14.5 cm. diam. **£280-340**

A pair of Barr Worcester ice-pails, covers and liners, painted in the manner of Thomas Baxter against an orange ground, richly gilt, incised B marks, 36 cm. high, c. 1800. **£5,300-5,900**

A pair of Barr Worcester flowerpots and stands, with fixed gilt ring handles painted with river landscapes within gilt rectangular cartouches reserved on a pink band, the stands incised 13, c. 1805, 17.5 cm. high overall. **£450-600**

A Worcester blue and white sparrow beak jug, decorated with the 'Three Flowers' pattern, c. 1775, 4¼ in. high. **£110-140**

A good Royal Worcester jardiniere, painted and signed by Ricketts, with a moulded burnished gilt border, 8¼ in., purple printed mark including the date code for 1925. **£400-500**

A Royal Worcester pierced and double-walled goblet, 19 cm., printed and impressed crowned circle marks, date code for 1875 **£300-400**

A Dr. Wall moulded bellied cream jug with cover, with Worcester Japan pattern, 5¼ in. high. **£560-620**

A pair of unusual Royal Worcester lampstands, after the originals by James Hadley, coloured in muted shades of apricot, olive-green and brown with gilt details, chips, one base restored, 59.5 cm., printed crowned circle, Rd. No. 67079/80, Trade Mark 'Cricklite' 1202, impressed P10, date code for 1903. **£700-900**

A pair of Worcester Chinoiserie tankards, each painted in colours with Chinoiserie figures on terraces and in pavilions about 9 cm. high, c. 1760. **£600-£800**

A fine and early Worcester small mug, painted in underglaze blue with the 'Warbler' pattern, 7.7 cm., TF mark, c. 1755. **£800-£1,000**

A rare Worcester bell-shaped mug, printed in black by Robert Hancock, 8.5 cm. First Period. **£950-1,100**

A First Period blue and white Worcester tankard, printed with the 'Plantation' pattern, c. 1765, 4½ in. high. **£180-200**

A First Period Worcester blue and white mug, c. 1765, 5 in. high. **£260-290**

A Worcester polychrome mug, decorated with the 'Long Eliza' pattern, c. 1770, 5 in. high. **£460-£500**

A Worcester tankard, with scroll handle, painted with the 'Jabberwocky' pattern beneath a turquoise border edged with gilt C scrolls with pendant iron-red flowers, c. 1770, 16.5 cm. high. **£400-500**

A First Period Worcester cylindrical mug, printed in black by Robert Hancock, with a half length portrait of the Marquis of Granby, flanked by Fame and Minerva, 8.4 cm. **£450-550** *This print is taken from an engraving by Richard Houston after Joshua Reynolds.*

A Worcester black transfer mug, by Hancock, with chip, 3½ in. high. **£150-175.** Perfect: **£200-£250**

A Dr. Wall Worcester scale blue tankard, decorated with English flowers, 3½ in. high. **£850-930**

A Grainger's Worcester hand-painted mug, with 'A present from a friend', 4 in. high, c. 1820. **£210-240**

A very rare Worcester transfer printed mug, printed in black by Sadler with a bust portrait of Queen Charlotte, slight rubbing to print, 4¾ in., c. 1763. **£2,100-£2,600**

87

A Worcester shell-painted plaque, with a gold border applied with white beading, painted in colours, mounted in silver to form a card tray, 14.5 cm. by 30 cm. overall, the silver by Richard Garrard, London, 1848, the porcelain earlier but unmarked, probably Barr, Flight & Barr. **£600-800**

A Barr Flight & Barr Piggin, painted on one side with peasant figures in a landscape, the reverse with a vignette depicting a rustic carrying a bundle of faggots, 2¾ in., early 19th C. **£200-250**

A Royal Worcester 'Japonaise' porcelain pilgrim bottle, the whole heightened in bronze, gold and shades of brown, puce printed mark and date '1874', 32.5 cm. **£360-420**
A fine example of the Aesthetic Movement of the 1870's and 80's.

A Royal Worcester circular plaque, painted by James Stinton, signed, with pheasants standing on the edge of a wood, 10.5 cm., date code for 1922, in original glazed gilt frame. **£200-£250**

A Dr. Wall Worcester scale blue plate, decorated with birds, 8 in. wide. **£500-560**

A First Period Worcester gros blue scalloped rim plate, with English flowers, c. 1760-70, 7½ in. wide. **£310-350**

A First Period Worcester scalloped plate, with apple green border and English flowers, 9 in. wide, c. 1775. **£235-265**

A pair of Worcester plates, painted in the atelier of James Giles in colours with gilt scalloped rims, red anchor marks, c. 1760, 19 cm. diam. **£400-600**

A Worcester Dr. Wall lobed plate, from the Earl Manvers service, 8¼ in. diam., c. 1770. **£450-500**

A Worcester polychrome scalloped rim plate, decorated with English flowers, c. 1770, 7½ in. diam. **£155-185**

A Worcester 'Blind Earl' polychrome plate, c. 1760, 7½ in. diam. **£300-330**
The so-called 'Blind Earl' pattern was named after the Earl of Coventry who lost his sight in a hunting accident. It is said that the pattern was made to stand out from the surface so that the Earl could feel the pattern. The pattern in fact pre-dates that mishap.

A rare Worcester deep plate, from the Duke of Gloucester service, 25 cm., gilded crescent mark, about 1768-71. **£1,500-£1,700**

89

A Worcester fable plate, by
Fidele Duvivier, c. 1770, 8 in.
wide. **£540-600**

A First Period Worcester
polychrome plate, with English
flowers and birds, c. 1775, 9 in.
wide. **£380-440**

A Worcester plate, black transfer
print by Hancock, c. 1780, 9 in.
diam. **£140-160**

A Worcester blue and white
plate, decorated with the 'Pine
Cone' pattern, 8¼ in. diam.,
c. 1780, slight chip: **£50-60.**
Perfect: **£100-130**

A Davis, Flight Worcester plate,
painted with Prince of Wales
plumes, from a service presented
to George III on visiting factory,
c. 1784. **£110-130**

A Worcester Flight Barr and
Barr armorial plate, with deep
burgundy ground, c. 1825,
8½ in. **£140-160**

A set of 6 Royal Worcester
dessert plates, painted by T.
Lockyer, signed, with shaped gilt
rim, 22.5 cm., printed crowned
circle, retailer's mark for Maple,
date code for 1933. **£700-800**

A Worcester Flight Barr and
Barr plate, for the Imaum of
Muscat, with a scene of Prince
Regent entering Muscat cove,
pale lime green ground, gadroon
border, 1836, 10½ in. **£220-240**

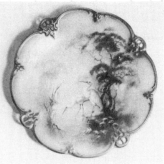

A Royal Worcester James
Hadley plate, painted and signed
by Powell, 8½ in. **£200-220**

A Royal Worcester pot pourri
vase and covers, painted and
signed by Ricketts, 8¼ in.,
purple printed mark including
the date code for 1889. **£350-500**

A Royal Worcester pot pourri
vase and cover, painted with
coloured flower sprays, edged in
gilding, reserved on a graduated
peach and ivory coloured ground,
wood stand, 12 in., purple
printed marks, workman's
marks, 1920. **£300-400**

A Worcester blue and white
sauceboat, painted with a
fisherman in a boat by a river
island and another crossing a
bridge, the interior with
scattered trailing branches,
three minute rim chips, painter's
mark, c. 1754, 15 cm. wide. **£400-
£500**

A pair of Worcester cos lettuce
leaf-moulded sauceboats, picked
out in brown, pink and yellow,
painted with flower sprays
within chocolate line rims, one
foot cracked, both rims with
minute chips, c. 1755, 22 cm.
long. **£300-400**

WORCESTER

A Worcester sauceboat, painted with a stag hunt and figures at discussion among trees and by pavilions in rocky landscapes within foliage-moulded cartouches, the interior with a green diaper-pattern border reserved with flowers, slight chip to rim and foot, c. 1754, 18 cm. wide. **£300-400**

A Flight Barr and Barr scent bottle, c. 1815, 4 in. high. **£500-£580**

A Worcester blue and white sucrier and cover, c. 1765, 5 in. high. **£315-355**

A Worcester blue and white saucer, workman's mark, 5¾ in. diam. c. 1768 **£75-85**

A Worcester blue and white saucer, with fruit pattern, with blue rim, transfer print, 5 in. diam. c. 1780-90. **£25.** Teabowl and saucer: **£45-60**

A Worcester blue and white spoon tray, c. 1770, 6½ in. wide. **£180-200**

A First Period Worcester 'Dry Blue' sucrier and cover, 5 in. high, c. 1790. **£400-450**
The major output of the Worcester factory was confined to underglaze blue. It is quite rare to find overglaze blue enamelling.

A Worcester painted
'Cannonball' teabowl and saucer,
c. 1765. **£90-100**

A Worcester blue and white
teabowl and saucer, with 'Three
Flowers' pattern, c. 1765. **£55-65**

A Dr. Wall Worcester teabowl
and saucer, decorated with an
oriental scene, c. 1770. **£150-175**

A Worcester powder blue
teabowl and saucer, 1760-70.
£280-360

A Worcester teacup and saucer,
decorated with the 'Jabberwocky'
pattern, well painted with an
exotic dragon-like bird in a
Japanese landscape within a
scrolling turquoise ground
border, c. 1760-70. **£100-150**

A Worcester teabowl and saucer, painted with iron-red and yellow flowerheads and with turquoise foliage, c. 1768. **£130-160**

A First Period Worcester teacup and saucer, with 'marriage pattern', note arrow through flowers, c. 1770. **£450-500**

A late First Period Worcester teacup and saucer, painted in the Meissen style in puce camaïeu, cup with crossed swords and 9 mark in underglaze blue. **£100-£150**

A Worcester teabowl and saucer, with turquoise and gilt border, c. 1770. **£90-105**

A Worcester teacup and saucer, painted in Kakiemon palette, pseudo seal marks in underglaze blue, c. 1770. **£280-360** *Japanese patterns were very popular during the later years of First Period Worcester.*

A Worcester blue and white trio, 'Immortelle' pattern, c. 1780. **£145-165**

A Flight Barr and Barr teacup and saucer, on apricot ground with gilding, c. 1814. **£50-60**

A Flight, Davis trio, 1780. **£60-£75**
A typical example of neo-classical influenced porcelain, with characteristic spiral fluting and restrained formal wreaths.

A Worcester hand-painted blue and white teacup and saucer, feather moulded, c. 1768. **£95-£115**

A Worcester teabowl, coffee cup and saucer, printed in black and coloured in overglaze enamels with 'Les Garcons Chinois', c. 1760. **£500-600**

A First Period Worcester polychrome painted teapot, c. 1770, 5¼ in. **£135-155**

A Worcester teacup, coffee cup and saucer from a marriage service, painted with sprays of flowers, crescent mark, c. 1780. **£275-375**

A First Period Worcester teapoy with cover, c. 1775, 6¼ in. **£235-£285**

A Worcester gros bleu ground tea caddy and a cover, painted with exotic birds among trees and butterflies within gilt fan-shaped C-scroll cartouches, c. 1770, 17 cm. high overall. **£800-£1,000**

95

WORCESTER

A Worcester blue and white coffee pot and cover, minute chip to spout, blue crescent mark, c. 1765, 21.5 cm. high. **£400-460**

A Worcester 'Immortelle Pattern' part tea and coffee service, painted in underglaze blue, comprising: coffee pot and cover, a teapot and cover and 6 teabowls and saucers, coffee pot 22.2 cm. high, teapot: 13.6 cm., open crescent marks, about 1765-70, rim of coffee pot cover chipped, both knops chipped. **£1,200-1,500**
This pattern is also called the 'Meissen onion' pattern and 'Copenhagen' pattern.

A Royal Worcester tea kettle and cover, in green, yellow, bronze and gold, impressed marks, late 19th C. **£150-200**

A Dr. Wall Worcester blue and white teapot and cover, decorated with the 'Fence' pattern, C. mark, in good condition, c. 1765. **£235-260**

A Worcester globular teapot and cover, painted in the Imari style, minute chips to spout and finial, c. 1770, 18.5 cm. wide. **£200-260**

A First Period Worcester blue and white 'Mansfield Pattern' teapot, c. 1770, 4¾ in. high. **£325-365**

Worcester polychrome teapot, 1775, 5 in. **£315-350**

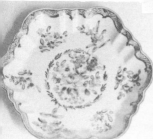

First Period Worcester polychrome teapot and stand, with a 'Compagnie des Indes' pattern, c. 1770. **£220-250** *It was only towards the end of the First Period that Worcester made direct copies of Chinese exportware.*

A Royal Worcester 'Fearful Consequences — through the laws of Natural Selection and Evolution — of living up to one's teapot' teapot and cover, spout restored, chips, 15.8 cm., printed mark, title, registration mark, 'Budge' and date code for 1882. **£200-300**

A Royal Worcester tray, with fluted rim, painted in sepia, raised and tooled gilding and silver lustre, 15 in., purple printed and impressed marks, gilder's initials SW, 1883. **£100-£200**

Three Flight, Barr & Barr Worcester pierced campana-shaped vases, minor chips to underside of rims, impressed and printed marks, c. 1825, 34 cm. high. **£1,600-2,000**

A Worcester blue and white bottle vase, with garlic neck, painted with Chinoiserie figures, script blue W mark, c. 1760, 26 cm. high. **£1,000-1,400**

A Dr. Wall Worcester colour transfer vase, c. 1760. **£400-440**

A pair of Royal Worcester vases, in several shades of gilding against a cream ground, 24.2 cm., printed crowned circle, c. 1885. **£200-300**

A rare Worcester vase, painte[in underglaze blue in the manner of James Rogers, 17.5 cm., painter's mark, abo[1760. **£2,600-3,000**

A Royal Worcester pierced vase in mauve and green, with rich enamel 'jewelling' and gilding, chips, 20 cm., printed crowned circle and indistinct date code, c. 1880. **£250-300**
All Worcester factories produced pierced or reticulated wares beginning with Chamberlains in the 1840's.

A Royal Worcester vase and cover, painted by Charles Baldwyn, signed, on a matt turquoise ground, 17 cm., shape no. 1515, date code for 1902. **£450-600**

INDEX